OXFORD MEDICAL PUBLICATIONS

Migraine

THE FACTS

The Visions of Hildegard (1098–1179). Some of the 'visions' bear a striking resemblance to the visual features of a migraine attack. (Reproduced from Singer: *From Magic to Science* (reprinted 1958) by kind permission of Dover Publications Inc.)

Migraine

THE FACTS

BY

F. CLIFFORD ROSE

AND

M. GAWEL

Charing Cross Hospital, London

OXFORD
OXFORD UNIVERSITY PRESS
NEW YORK   TORONTO   MELBOURNE
1979

Oxford University Press, Walton Street, Oxford OX2 6DP

OXFORD LONDON GLASGOW
NEW YORK TORONTO MELBOURNE WELLINGTON
IBADAN NAIROBI DAR ES SALAAM LUSAKA CAPE TOWN
KUALA LUMPUR SINGAPORE JAKARTA HONG KONG TOKYO
DELHI BOMBAY CALCUTTA MADRAS KARACHI

© F. Clifford Rose and M. Gawel 1979

British Library Cataloguing in Publication Data
Rose, Frank Clifford
    Migraine. – (Oxford medical publications).
    1. Migraine
    I. Title   II. Gawel, M   III. Series
    616.8'57   RC392   79–40892
    ISBN 0–19–261161–5

Typeset by Hope Services Ltd., Abingdon
Printed in Great Britain
by R. Clay & Co. Ltd., Bungay

Contents

1

What is migraine?

The word migraine comes from the Greek term for a one-sided headache (*he-micrain-ia*). But not all headaches are due to migraine and, since the treatment will depend on the cause, it is important to separate the different types of headache. Various types of migrainous headaches are described in this chapter, and in Chapter 2 we discuss some headaches that are not migraine.

Classical migraine

The classical descriptions of migraine gave three features of this particular type of headache: first, it was one-sided; secondly, it was accompanied by nausea and sometimes vomiting; and thirdly, there was a warning of a disturbance of vision.

Patient A.B. gave the following description:

I wake up in the morning feeling happy. The sky seems more blue—in fact, all colours appear more intense. I know this means that later that day, or perhaps the next, I will get a migraine attack. The pain gradually comes on over one temple, usually the right, and spreads over the whole of that side of the head. At the same time, but sometimes before the headache begins, part of my vision blurs, bright stars may appear and move over the field of vision. The headache becomes worse and throbbing, I start feeling sick. If I vomit this seems to make the headache better. With the headache, light hurts my eyes so I have to go to bed after drawing the curtains. The whole attack lasts about eight hours and leaves me tired and shaken.

This is a description of an attack of classical migraine. In addition to the three typical features (one-sided headache, nausea and vomiting, and visual disturbances), it includes other characteristics found with migrainous attacks.

Migraine

The warning

The warning of several hours, or a day or even two, before the actual attack is well known to many sufferers. Although in this case it took the form of feeling happy and being more aware of colours, there may be other variations in mood, increased energy, a feeling of hunger or thirst, or even just the feeling that something is about to happen. When hunger is the warning, over-eating can sometimes prevent the attack.

This period probably stems from a chemical imbalance in those areas of the brain which control mood and emotion. One such area, the hypothalamus, controls the secretion of several hormones and it is possible that an alteration in its setting may be a trigger for the ensuing headache.

The headache

Pain over the temple is usually the first sign, followed by its spread to one side of the head (see Fig. 1.1). The pain may then spread over the whole of the head. This pain is due to the widening (dilatation) of the blood vessels to the head and the characteristic throbbing sensation is due to the pulse affecting these dilated blood vessels. The headache can last as long as 24 hours but often no more than six or eight hours (as in patient A.B.); sometimes the sufferer is lucky enough to fall asleep to discover on waking that the headache has gone.

Visual symptoms

It is very common during a migraine headache to find light troublesome and disturbing (photophobia) whilst darkness is soothing.

Blurred vision is also frequent but the most characteristic visual symptom is an inability to see out of part of the visual field. The visual abnormalities can take different forms and be very dramatic (see Figs. 1.1–1.8). The whole visual field may be fragmented and interrupted by shiny lines, arranged

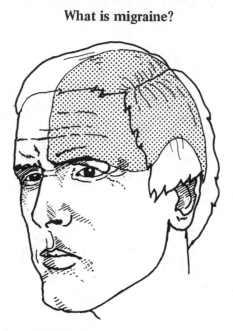

Fig. 1.1. Classical migraine: only one side of the head aches

like constellations, a phenomenon known as fortification spectra, because of its resemblance to a castellated fort. (Some mystics have interpreted these as visions of 'the eternal city'.) There may also be small multicoloured areas of flashing lights, zigzag patterns, or 'Catherine wheels', and there is usually generalized blurring of vision, as if looking through steam or water. Another common visual feature is loss of the vision either in a roughly circular area, or in half of a visual field, i.e. the area seen to one side. (Just as one side of the body is controlled by the opposite half of the brain, the area of space perceived on one side is a function of the opposite side of the brain; this means that damage of the visual area of the left half of the brain produces a loss in vision of the right half of the visual fields of *both* eyes. Such a blacking-out during a migraine attack implies that one hemisphere of the brain is affected.)

Less common disturbances of perception are changes in

Fig. 1.2. Bright shimmering 'stars' seen falling across the image (teichopsia) (cf. Fig. 1.5)

the size and the shape of objects, the appearance that objects are tilted or far away or that colours have faded. (These changes are due to alteration in blood flow to the parietal lobes of the brain, which deal with orientation in space and time.)

Migrainous patients sometimes complain that they feel taller, or are 'about one foot high'. At one time it was thought that Lewis Carroll, a migraine sufferer, was drawing on his own experience of such sensations in *Alice in Wonderland*, but this intriguing explanation was somewhat discredited by the later suggestion that he wrote this book *before* he developed migrainous symptoms.

The visual disturbances (aura) usually herald the onset of headache but occasionally occur later in the attack. Rarely the headache itself plays only a small part in the attack, as in the following case.

Fig. 1.3. Scintillating scotoma: an area of loss of vision surrounded by a bright starburst; this often moves across the field of vision

Patient C.D., a 42-year-old physician, was driving along Regent Street during the rush-hour to an appointment for which he was late. He suddenly found he could not read the licence-plate of the car immediately in front of him. He had never suffered from migrainous symptoms previously. After about 30 seconds the blind spot (scotoma) began to alter, opening up to form an enlarging crescent of shimmering angles which spread to the periphery of the visual field and disappeared. This phenomenon—a typical migrainous aura—lasted precisely 20 minutes and was followed by irritability and lack of appetite lasting a few hours, but no headache was noticed.

There is little doubt that these symptoms were migrainous in origin in spite of the absence of headache, i.e. the cause was a narrowing (spasm) of the blood vessels (vasoconstriction) feeding the brain, so that less blood flowed to it.

Other manifestations of the narrowing of these blood vessels are transient weakness and numbness, or even loss of consciousness. The weakness, which can be as severe as that

5

Fig. 1.4. Bright-edged, castellated line (fortification spectrum)

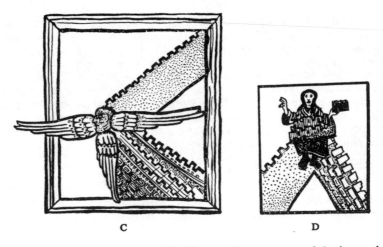

C

D

Fig. 1.5. From the Visions of Hildegard: 'The ramparts of the heavenly city'

Fig. 1.6. Loss, blanking or darkening of one half of the field of vision (hemianopia)

which occurs in stroke, may continue after the headache has gone; in a very small minority, the diminution in blood flow may be so severe that permanent damage of the brain results in permanent weakness.

Other people report changes in auditory perception, for instance speech may sound as though it is being played at too fast a speed. Sounds may seem overwhelmingly loud, or continue to reverberate after they have ceased.

Rarely, a sufferer may feel there is another person looking on—the *döppelganger*.

Migraine sufferers often do not mention such odd sensations and perceptions for fear of being thought 'insane' but all these phenomena are consistent with a migrainous aura due to vasoconstriction.

Fig. 1.7. Fragmentation of the visual image

Fig. 1.8. Tunnel vision. The visual image appears smaller and more distant, as if viewed down the wrong end of a telescope

What is migraine?

Common migraine

Only a minority of sufferers have visual aura or other features of vasoconstriction and often the headache is not one-sided. These headaches, which are just as frequent as classical migraine, are called common migraine and are otherwise similar.

There are other types of headache which are also included under the general umbrella term of migraine but which differ from classical or common migraine in several respects.

Migrainous neuralgia (cluster headaches)

Patient E.F., a 35-year-old insurance salesman, described an attack as follows:

I am woken in the early hours of the morning by an intense pain behind my left eye, as if someone was sticking a red hot needle into it. I get out of bed to find my nose feels blocked and the left eye is watering. When I look in the mirror, the eye is red. The attack lasts half an hour and goes as quickly as it came. The extraordinary thing is that the attack occurs every night at 2 or 3 a.m. and this has been going on for nearly three weeks.

This is a typical example of migrainous neuralgia. Men are affected more often than women (in the proportion of about 10:1) and it usually occurs between the ages of 30 and 50 years. The sufferer is often woken at night by a very severe pain behind one eye, described often as crushing, lancing like a 'hot poker', or stabbing (Fig. 1.9). There is often watering of the affected eye, which is reddened, and the nostril on that side becomes stuffy and may even run. The attack may last for half an hour and then go, only to return the following night at the same time. The episodes last several weeks and, for this reason, other names (and there are twenty!) include the term 'cluster headaches'. The cluster may occur two or three times a year or only once in two or three years.

9

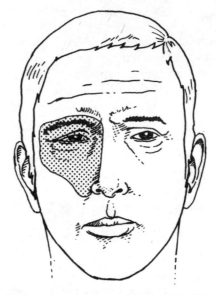

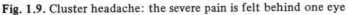

Fig. 1.9. Cluster headache: the severe pain is felt behind one eye

Facial migraine

In some patients the pain of migraine is felt in the face, either in a distribution similar to that found in cluster headaches or lower down the cheek. In these cases, the pain is less severe, less sharp, and may last for a much longer time than in a classical or common migraine attack.

Basilar migraine

This usually occurs in young women. The headache is commonly over the back of the head and, besides nausea, the symptoms may include giddiness, double vision, unsteadiness, and slurred speech. Perhaps the most alarming symptom is loss of consciousness. These symptoms are due to a diminished blood supply to parts of the brain supplied by the basilar

10

artery, a blood vessel at the base of the brain which goes into spasm to produce an attack.

Hemiplegic migraine

This is a very rare form in which there is a paralysis of the arm and leg on one side of the body. Fortunately the paralysis is temporary but it may be repeated. There is often a strong family history of similar attacks.

Ophthalmoplegic migraine

This, too, is rare and occurs particularly in children. During the attack, the eyelid droops, the pupil dilates, and the eye squints outward. Again these features are temporary and usually go when the headache stops.

Abdominal migraine

This occurs more commonly in women and its onset is usually in childhood. The pain is often over the upper part of the abdomen and lasts a few hours. The diagnosis is revealed by the family history of migraine and the occasional attacks in which the pain is preceded by about an hour of migraine, more commonly classical than common.

2

Headaches that are not migraine

Tension headaches

Tension headaches are caused by a tightening of the muscles at the back of the neck with consequent tension of the scalp (Fig. 2.1). The pain can be felt at the back of the neck, over the top of the head, or over the forehead, and is often described as a 'vice round the head' (Fig. 2.2). The tension of the muscles is in itself painful, but associated constriction of the arteries to the muscles make the pain considerably worse. The electromyograph (a machine which picks up electrical

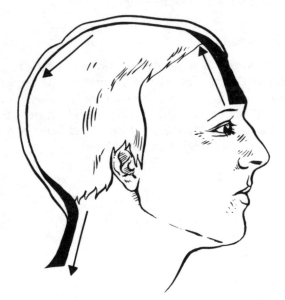

Fig. 2.1. Muscle-contraction (tension) headache: the muscles at the back of the neck become tense to pull on the scalp and stretch the forehead muscles.

12

activity in muscle) can prove that active muscle contraction occurs during this form of headache.

Patient G.H., a 45-year-old housewife, said:

For the past nine months, I have suffered from almost continuous headaches. It is as if I have a heavy weight on the top of my head and I notice it as soon as I wake in the morning. It lasts all day but it does not keep me awake at night although it is there when I wake up in the

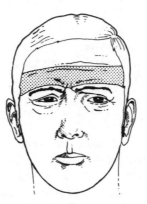

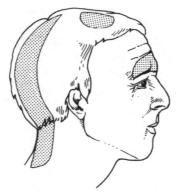

Fig. 2.2. Anxiety (tension) headache: the headache is felt like a tight band round the head; the pain may also be felt in the back of the neck and on top of the head.

morning. I do not feel sick and have no trouble with my eyes. Sometimes I feel a tight band around my head and usually the back of my neck feels stiff.

This is a typical tension or muscle-contraction headache. In the case of G.H., direct questioning revealed that the headaches had started after her husband had told her he was contemplating divorce but had not yet decided to leave the conjugal home. These sort of headaches could be due to depression, coupled as they were with feelings of lack of wanting to do anything, and early morning waking.

Anxiety-depressive headaches are commoner than typical migraine but the two types often occur at different times in the same sufferer.

Inflammatory diseases

When micro-organisms invade the body a battle ensues between them and the body's defences. White blood cells are mobilized and some of them release active substances into the local circulation. A similar release of active substances occurs during allergic reactions, or when a weal of a blister following a burn forms on the skin. These substances cause intense pain, as well as an increased sensitivity to pain; they can be divided into two groups, *kinins* which are derived from protein breakdown, and *amines*, especially *histamine*, which causes more inflammation and makes blood vessel walls porous, to produce swelling and redness.

Sinusitis

This pain often affects the area over the eye (frontal sinus) or below it (maxillary sinus) (see Fig. 2.3). The pain often comes on after a cold which blocks the nose and occurs each day, being worse in the afternoons. The pain is caused by inflammation and stretching of the periosteum and vessels by pus under tension. The area is often tender to pressure or tapping and the diagnosis can be confirmed by X-rays.

Headaches that are not migraine

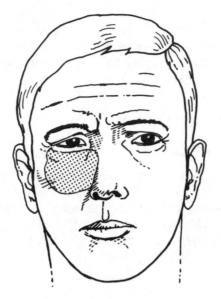

Fig. 2.3. Sinusitis: pain over the affected (maxillary) sinus

Meningitis

This is an inflammation of the brain's coverings (meninges) and is always associated with headache. The intense pain from the head gives rise to contraction of the muscles of the neck to produce the stiff neck which is a symptom of meningitis. It is a serious condition and when suspected, a spinal tap (lumbar puncture) is necessary to examine the cerebrospinal fluid. With modern antibiotics, over 90 per cent of cases should be cured.

Encephalitis

This means inflammation of the brain and is another very serious cause of headache.

15

Dental infection

This is sometimes a cause of headache but is more likely to cause pain in the jaws, and the lower more commonly than the upper.

Less common causes of headache

Trigeminal neuralgia

This affects people in the second half of life, affecting women twice as frequently as men. It consists of paroxysms of severe shooting or stabbing pains on one side of the face (see Fig. 2.4) which are brought on by shaving, eating, talking, or cold draughts. The painful spasms may last only a few seconds but can recur frequently.

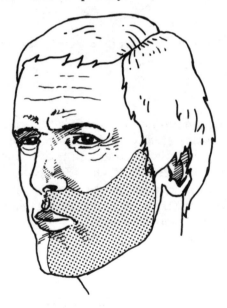

Fig. 2.4. Trigeminal neuralgia: the stabbing pain may affect any part of the face but usually the lower part.

Headaches that are not migraine

The cervical spine'

Abnormalities of this bone in the neck are often said to be the cause of headache. In fact this is the case much less commonly than supposed; anyone over the age of 50 years may have X-ray changes in the cervical spine but this does not necessarily mean they are the cause of the headaches.

There are many other less common causes of headache which come on after certain types of food but are not migrainous or allergic.

The Chinese restaurant syndrome

The symptoms come on within half an hour of starting a Chinese meal. Although headache, affecting chiefly the temples and forehead, is a feature, the chief complaints are of a feeling of tightness or pressure over the face and chest.

The offending substance has been found to be a chemical called monosodium glutamate. This compound is added to food to bring out its taste and the reason why Chinese food is often the culprit is because this substance is regularly added in relatively large quantities. It has also been found that three grams is enough to bring on the symptoms in susceptible subjects, particularly on an empty stomach. The syndrome is therefore more likely to occur after soup than after more solid food (absorption of the substance then being less rapid).

Hot-dog headache

Several people complain of headaches after eating cured meats of which hot-dog sausage is a classical example; others include bacon, ham, and salami. The headache comes on within half an hour of eating these foods and the offending substances are nitrites. These are well known vasodilators, producing flushing of the face. Nitrites are added to the salt

17

used in curing in order to give a uniform red colour to the meats.

Ice-cream headache

This headache is caused by holding very cold substances such as ice or ice-cream in the mouth. The intense cooling of the roof of the mouth produces a pain which is then referred to the head.

Alcohol

Alcohol is a powerful vasodilator, as evidenced by the flushed face of the inebriate. For this reason, it can produce a headache at the time of imbibition. But the term hangover is restricted to those symptoms, of which headache is predominant, which occur several hours later, usually the next day. It is almost certainly due to the breakdown products produced when alcohol is metabolized, including substances such as acetates and acetaldehyde.

Exertional headache

With exercise, the muscles require more blood so that there is generalized vasodilatation. This is why the face becomes flushed during exercise. The blood pressure also rises and this combination causes further stretching of the dilated intracranial blood vessels which can cause headache.

Headache associated with sexual intercourse is an example of exercise headache. It occurs at or near the time of orgasm and can be very severe. Although the pain lasts only a few minutes it can persist after intercourse and last for days. It affects women as well as men. Since the blood pressure can rise more than 50 per cent and the pulse rate double during intercourse, it is surprising that this type of headache is not more common.

Headaches that are not migraine

High blood pressure

Probably the commonest cause of headache in those with high blood pressure (hypertension) is anxiety over their blood pressure. But there is no doubt that marked ('malignant') hypertension can cause severe headache along with other neurological disturbances (hypertensive encephalopathy). Patients with both migraine and high blood pressure often find that when the blood pressure is brought down to normal levels, the intensity and frequency of the migraine attacks lessen.

Strokes

There are two main types of stroke depending on whether the blood vessel to the brain bleeds (cerebral haemorrhage) or is blocked (cerebral infarction). Patients with cerebral haemorrhage nearly always have a headache, particularly if the blood gets into the space surrounding the brain (subarachnoid haemorrhage). This bleeding often arises from a weakened part of a blood vessel which has ballooned out forming an *aneurysm*, or occasionally from an abnormal congenital group of blood vessels—an *angioma*. Whatever the cause, the symptoms are usually typical: a sudden pain is felt across the head as if the patient had been struck with a hammer; loss of consciousness may follow. The headache subsequently persists and the irritation of the meninges causes a picture resembling meningitis.

Temporal arteritis

This produces a very severe headache, usually in older people over the age of 55 years. The arteries in the temples can be seen to be more thickened and tortuous and they are particularly tender. The sufferer is generally unwell and may have had pains all over the body (polymyalgia rheumatica) for weeks with loss of appetite and loss of weight. The diagnosis

19

is easily made by doing a simple blood test with confirmation by examining a small piece of the temporal artery under the microscope (and finding 'giant-cells'). Early diagnosis is important in this condition because a major complication is blindness. The headache disappears completely following treatment with steroids.

Brain tumour

Of all the causes of headache, this is the one that most patients and doctors fear most. In fact, it occurs only in a very small minority of headache sufferers and can often be recognized by the characteristics of the headache.

The history is usually of short duration e.g. less than three months, but of increasing severity. The headache is made worse by coughing, sneezing, and bending down (but this can also occur in benign headaches). The headache may wake the patient from sleep and tends to be worse in the morning. There is often associated morning nausea or vomiting.

Other ominous symptoms include drowsiness, yawning, or hiccup. If there are neurological signs present, then further investigation is mandatory.

Benign headaches

These occur frequently and have no serious significance. Two types of these have recently been described by Dr. John Pearce: The 'exploding head' occurs in middle aged or elderly people, most often women. It always occurs at night when the sufferer is woken up with a painful sensation as if a forceful explosion has taken place in the head. Although the sensation soon goes, it leaves the person with a sense of fear, sweating, and rapid pulse rate. The 'needle-in-the-eye' syndrome is more common and feels like a sharp jab with a needle in the corner of the eye. It lasts only a matter of seconds and can recur several times a day.

3

Who gets migraine?

Migraine is far from being a trivial disorder, not least because the problems posed by migraine in the community and in the family can be enormous.

Migraine cost the National Health Service £2.8 million in 1970, consisting of pharmaceutical costs of £1.6 million, general practice expenses of £0.7 million, and hospital investigations of £0.5 million. Private treatment, and remedies bought privately, add further to this. In 1968–9, 295 000 man-days and 167 000 woman-days were lost from work on account of migraine. This, too, is an under-estimate since the calculation is based on health certificates which are issued only after three days off work, and most sufferers from migraine are often away for less than this at any one time. A recent survey showed that 21 per cent of Members of Parliament have migraine and that each one lost an average four man-days a year. Those who persist in working during an attack are likely to be less efficient, which also contributes to the problems caused by migraine.

Nearly everyone has a headache at some time in their lives but migraine with its special features affects only a minority. Estimates vary, depending on how migraine is defined, but it probably affects over 10 per cent of men and over 20 per cent of women. The reason as to why it should be commoner in women is not precisely known but this sex difference could be one more clue as to the cause.

The age at which migraine begins is also variable. It usually starts in adolescents and young adults but many of these have warnings as children of its likely development.

Migraine

Migraine in children

It is more usual for children to have common migraine than classical attacks with visual symptoms; these become more frequent in the teenage group. Children suffer from conditions called migraine equivalents which often take the form of periodic (cyclical) vomiting not due to any obvious cause such as over-indulgence of food. These 'bilious attacks' can occur once monthly but last no more than a day.

Recurrent abdominal pain with, or without, vomiting is another warning that the child may develop migrainous headaches on growing up. Children who are more prone to travel sickness than others are a further group with a tendency to develop migraine in later life.

In all these cases, a clue as to the true nature of the condition will often be found in the family because there is very likely to be a close relative with migrainous headaches.

Although more women than men suffer from migraine, in children, boys are just as likely to have symptoms as girls.

Heredity

There is no doubt that migraine is a familial disorder. Estimates of how frequently it runs in families will depend on how widely the term 'family' is extended. Even restricted to close (first-degree) relatives such as parents, siblings and children, it is still over 50 per cent more common within than outside the family. Indeed, a positive family history of migraine is further evidence that a headache sufferer has migraine.

The precise way in which migraine is inherited is not as simple as, for example, the inheritance of blood groups. Nor is it scientific to say that headaches are inherited, but only the tendency to have certain types of headaches.

Other familial disorders, such as allergy and epilepsy, have been said to be commoner in migrainous families but there is no scientific proof of this.

22

Who gets migraine?

The migrainous personality

Since the eighteenth century, doctors have thought that it was the 'upper' strata of society that suffered more from migraine. In those days it would only have been the better-off that could have afforded doctors' fees. Recent scientific studies indicate that migraine attacks occur in all ranks, irrespective of intelligence. The reason why the myth has persisted for two centuries is because of the biased selection of patients that doctors see; there is no doubt that only a minority of migraine sufferers go to their doctor. These groups are more likely to be those with more money, time, or intelligence. This applies to other 'complainers' and not simply migraine sufferers.

It has also been thought that hard-working, conscientious perfectionists are more likely to suffer from migraine, a subjective view that migrainous doctors find hard to dispute. The objective studies that have been done do not confirm that one type of personality is more prone than others and show that migraine occurs just as frequently in people who are neither obsessional nor compulsive.

There is no doubt that some migraine sufferers are aggressive, demanding, and distrustful. An explanation for this could well be that any person suffering from repeated headaches is likely to become 'neurotic' or depressed. It can be difficult to decide whether these characteristics are the result or the cause of migraine.

There is little doubt that stress of various sorts can predispose to migraine attacks, and this is discussed more fully in later chapters.

Relationship of migraine to other diseases

Although there are many conditions that produce pain in the head region, e.g. sinusitis, high blood pressure, eye strain, there is no proof that these conditions predispose to migraine.

On the other hand, many migraine sufferers notice that

their attacks are more frequent when they are 'run-down' or suffering from general upsets.

Case C.D. (mentioned in Chapter 1), on returning from a lecture-tour of India, suddenly developed frequent (sometimes twice-daily) attacks of migraine, which were produced by slight stress, e.g. a short walk. Analysis of his blood showed evidence of an infection, which later proved to be an inflammatory bowel disorder. When the latter condition was cured with treatment, he suffered no further migraine attacks.

Migraine in the elderly

Old people do not suffer from migraine as commonly or as severely as the young. There are exceptions to this rule, however. Many women whose migraine is worse at the time of the menstrual period are told that their attacks will go with the menopause. This is often, but not always, the case.

There is little doubt that, on the whole, attacks change in their characteristics with ageing, e.g. vomiting is less severe and in many cases the disorder becomes less troublesome.

Weekend migraine

Although migraine is often thought of as a stress disease, there are many sufferers who get attacks only when they are relaxing either at weekends or on holiday. Others will get attacks only when they are anticipating an exciting event, e.g. a party. This can be so distinctive that they will refuse invitations in the certain knowledge that acceptance will provoke an attack.

4

Why does the head ache?

Since almost everyone suffers from headache at some time, it is often not regarded as a disease, although clearly it is 'disease' (i.e. not being at ease). But since headache interferes considerably with the lives of significant numbers of people, it seems illogical to regard it as normal. However, the changes occurring in the body are subtle, so that it is exceedingly difficult to analyse changes taking place, even with sophisticated research tools. Often, no sooner has some abnormality been discovered, than it is shown to be only secondary to pain, or not to be present in all who supposedly have the same symptoms. By comparison, the understanding of an obvious abnormality such as an infected chest is simple, as not only can changes be seen on an X-ray, but the 'cause' can be isolated by observing the germ in the laboratory.

The fact that a number of people have a specific form of headache does not necessarily mean that the cause is the same in all of them. In the same way, a blocked nose and sore throat may be caused by infection with germs or by allergy; the symptoms can be identical but the treatment of each is very different. Treating a 'runny' nose due to hay fever with antibiotics is worse than useless.

The situation in the classification of headaches is analogous, except that a good deal is known about the structures concerned with pain and the nerves which carry the sensation.

The pathway of pain

There are pathways in the nervous system which help us appreciate our environment, whether by sight, touch, or hearing. Each sense organ can be regarded as an extension, or the sensitive area, of a nerve which is linked to the brain. In the case of the eyes, the light-sensitive cells in the back of the eyeball (retina) are linked together in specific patterns which are then transmitted by the optic nerves to a relay station at the base of the brain. In lower animals, much organization of incoming information is carried out here but, in man and other primates, most of the processing occurs in the grey matter of the brain, the cortex. Here, the shape perceived is compared with stored information and recognition occurs when the pattern is matched with memory. A label is supplied by an area of the brain concerned with memory and we have a conscious appreciation of what the object is. A similar process occurs with the recognition of sounds but, in this case, different areas of the brain are involved.

Touch (tactile sensation) is different in that the impulses have to travel a greater distance to the brain up the spinal cord (except in the case of sensation on the face). The other varieties of sensation besides touch include temperature, superficial pain, and deep pain. Impulses travel along nerve fibres from sensitive structures in the skin to the spinal cord where they relay with long nerve fibres grouped together. These travel to the brain where two things happen: the first is that the sensation is localized, because only that group of nerve fibres in the brain concerned solely with sensation from the specifically activated area is stimulated; secondly, other areas of the brain go into a state of expectancy, a general alerting reaction. Because of this activation (which can be measured electrically) there is an increased flow of blood to the nerve cells. Complex patterns of skin stimulation can be analysed in much the same way as patterns of light and sound perceived by eyes and ears.

The structures in the skin or other tissues which receive painful stimuli are of a specific type, and are different from those sensitive to touch and temperature. Pain sensation is served by two types of nerve fibre, fast and slow, each of which transmits pain of a different character: the fast fibre transmits discrete, sharp pain whilst the slow fibre produces dull and diffuse pain. Slow-conducting fibres also transmit

26

pain-killing (analgesic) drugs. The pain thresholds vary greatly and become unpredictable in subjects who are tired or anxious. Scientific, objective methods of measurement and analysis are very necessary in the study of what is, in the final analysis, a subjective complaint.

People tend to suppress the memory of unpleasant events and, for this reason, it is often difficult to give an accurate account of a previous pain. The suppression is partly due to unconscious forgetting, but partly because the chemicals produced by the pain dulls memory.

Response to pain is also to some extent dependent on sociological factors. People in social classes I and II are more likely to complain of headache, a tendency that has given the false impression that they are more prone to get headaches.

Brain substance itself is insensitive to pain; neurosurgeons can operate on it without general anaesthesia. The structures within the head that feel pain are the blood vessels and the coverings of the brain (the meninges). The pain felt in migranous headaches is due to pressure of swollen blood vessels against the sensitive membranes that sheath the skull.

The blood vessels and the brain

The brain is enclosed in a container of bone (the skull) which in turn is covered by a fibrous structure and skin (the scalp). The scalp is attached by muscles to the forehead and the bone of the neck so that tensing these muscles causes stretching of the scalp. Beneath the skin there are numerous blood vessels—arteries—taking blood from the heart and veins returning blood to it. The scalp arteries arise from the large carotid artery which divides in the neck into two branches (see Fig. 4.1). One of these, the external carotid artery, sends blood to the outside of the skull and also to the coverings of the brain (meninges) within the skull, whilst the other branch, the internal carotid artery, enters the skull to join with vessels originating from the vertebral artery. The blood supply to the brain is from branches of the left and right internal carotid

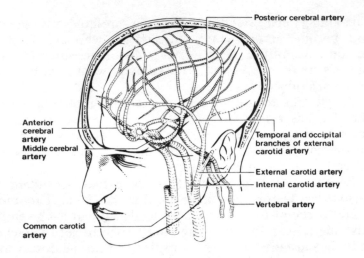

Fig. 4.1. The distribution of arteries inside and outside the skull. The internal carotid artery divides to form the anterior and middle cerebral arteries. The two vertebral arteries join to form the basilar artery which divides into the posterior cerebral arteries. The external carotid gives rise to numerous branches outside the skull, including the temporal and occipital arteries.

arteries which, with the vertebral arteries, form a communication round the base of the brain (the circle of Willis) (see Plate 1). From this circle, branches go to the front, centre, and back of the brain sending out a network of ever finer vessels which dive deep into the substance of the brain (see Plate 2).

Veins drain the blood from the brain and channel it into a series of large veins (venous sinuses) closely attached to the brain coverings (see Plate 3). From these, the blood travels either by way of the jugular veins, or by communications through the skull, to join with blood draining from the scalp to return eventually to the heart.

The coverings of the brain

The brain is enveloped by three coverings or meninges (see Fig. 4.2). The dura mater is the outer covering attached to

30

Why does the head ache?

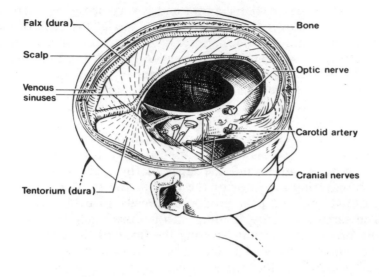

Falx (dura)

Scalp

Venous sinuses

Tentorium (dura)

Bone

Optic nerve

Carotid artery

Cranial nerves

Fig. 4.2. Pain sensitive structures in the skull. In this diagram the brain has been removed showing the pain sensitive supporting structures. The venous sinuses lie in the dura mater which stretches down the centre of the skull (the falx) and horizontally across the back of the skull (the tentorium).

the inside of the skull where in certain places it makes reinforcing sheets, e.g. the falx (a spine of dura running along the inside of the skull from front to back and separating the two cerebral hemispheres) and the tentorium which stretches across the back of the skull at the level of the ears and divides the cerebral hemispheres from the hind brain concerned with vital functions and balance.

Underlying the dura mater is the arachnoid mater which has beneath it a very fine layer that closely surrounds the brain and its blood vessels—the pia mater. Between the arachnoid and the pia is a fluid that bathes and protects the brain and spinal cord—the cerebrospinal fluid (CSF).

The skull itself has a covering (the periosteum), the inner structure of which is more porous and contains short blood vessels. The bone of the skull is insensitive to pain but the periosteum has pain receptors and is very sensitive, particularly in areas over the brow, temples, and at the back of the head; stretching of the periosteum, caused by inflammation or growths, will cause severe pain. Although the brain itself does not feel pain, all the main arteries supplying the dura and some of the smaller branches are sensitive, as are the blood vessels of the scalp, so the stretching of an artery on one side will cause severe pain on that side.

The dura above the tenorium, which divides the front and back of the brain, is entirely insensitive to pain, except near the venous sinuses and the areas of the main arteries. The dura covering the floor of the skull in the front area is very sensitive and the pain produced spreads to behind the eye. The same sensitivity is found in the dura lining the back of the brain but not that covering the floor of the areas below the temporal lobes. The falx is insensitive to pain in its front part except for just where it connects with the area above the nose.

Pressure on the tentorium produces pain in the area around the forehead and eye and ear on the same side. The great venous sinuses are very sensitive to pain but the smaller sinuses less so; interestingly, stimulation of the smaller sinuses at the back of the head causes pain over the forehead and eye.

The smaller arteries of the brain, as opposed to the main blood vessels, are insensitive to pain. The pain caused by dilatation of the internal carotid inside the skull is dull, throbbing, and eventually nauseating; it is localized behind the eye and over the temple on the same side as the stimulus.

Both distension and emptying of the brain ventricles causes pain; this explains the headache following spinal tap (lumbar puncture), where cerebrospinal fluid is removed for analysis.

The cranial nerves

There are twelve cranial nerves, the nerves that arise from the brain itself, but all the pain impulses in the head are carried

Why does the head ache?

by only two of these, the fifth and ninth cranial nerves, which also serve most of the other sensations felt in the head and face. Pain can also be produced by stimulating the tenth and eleventh cranial nerves, as well as nerves coming from the spinal cord in the upper part of the neck; this pain is felt at the back and top of the head.

The fifth or trigeminal nerve arises from an area in the upper part of the hind-brain and its control centre (nucleus) lies deep in the spinal cord in the neck. In this part of the nucleus the areas of the face are represented in a concentric way, so that damage to the upper part can cause tingling or loss of sensation round the lips. The main trunk of the nerve splits into three branches in an area of the skull near to the front of the upper part of the jaw bone. The upper branch goes to the area of face above the eye and forehead, the middle branch to the cheek, whilst the lower one goes to the lower jaw. There is, of course, an identical nerve on the other side of the face. When a dentist anaesthetizes half the jaw, it is a branch of this nerve that he is blocking.

Much of the knowledge regarding these pain pathways was ascertained by experiments on volunteers undergoing operations, since such a detailed analysis could not be obtained by work on animals; this speaks volumes for the co-operation and interest of the volunteers. Many of those who suffer from headaches are keenly interested in co-operating in research. The methods employed in these experiments varied, e.g. mild electric shocks and traction, but they were not the sort of stimuli that cause headaches in everyday life.

The sites within the head which give rise to pain are related to blood vessels, and the relationship between these and the structures they supply are of paramount importance (see Figs 4.1 and 4.2).

Blood vessels, especially arteries, have a muscular coat which enables them to change their diameter. These changes both alter the amount of, as well as the resistance to, blood flow. The smallest blood vessels (capillaries) form a network to supply organs with oxygen and nutrients, without which body tissues die. Blood flow to the tissues can also be regulated by opening or closing parts of the capillary system.

Pain due to stretching of blood vessels is the explanation of all vascular headaches, including migraine. The pulsation felt over the temple during an attack is due to dilatation of blood vessels and pressure on an artery, because it prevents or limits pulsations, lessens the pain. This is the way that an ice pack, by producing constriction of blood vessels, relieves an attack.

Before the headache phase of migraine, which is due to widening of blood vessels (vasodilatation) outside the skull, there is a narrowing of blood vessels (vasoconstriction) inside the head. Why this first phase occurs is not known but, during a migrainous attack, there may be a very low cerebral blood flow (similar to that following a stroke caused by blockage of a blood vessel).

The decrease in blood flow to the brain accounts for the visual symptoms and other odd sensations before an attack (see Fig. 4.3). During or soon after the decrease of flow in

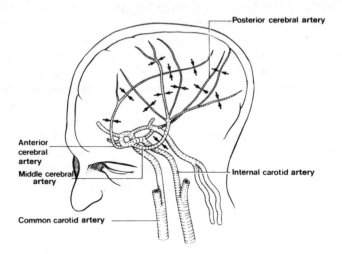

Fig. 4.3. During a migraine attack the branches of the internal carotid artery constrict (arrowed) causing neurological disturbances

Why does the head ache?

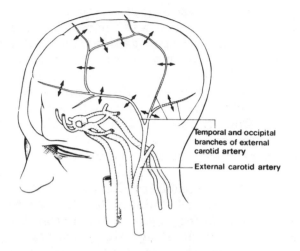

Fig. 4.4. Following the constriction shown in Fig. 4.3 the branches of the external carotid dilate (arrowed) causing the pain

the brain, there is a dilatation of the branches from the extra-cranial carotid artery and this marks the start of the headache (Fig. 4.4). The throbbing pain is made worse by the release of chemical substances (kinins and histamine). Nausea supervenes and this also occurs when the vessels are dilated passively. This simplistic explanation of the sequence of events in a severe attack of migraine gives a picture of the complex changes involved.

The autonomic nervous system

The muscle coats of blood vessels are supplied by nerves which, unlike those relaying pain sensations, have functions similar to those of nerves going to other muscle fibres; stimulation causes the muscle to contract and so narrow the blood vessels.

These particular nerves come from part of the nervous system which, because it deals with functions not usually under control of the conscious mind, is called the autonomic nervous system. This system is in two parts, the sympathetic and parasympathetic, each of which have different actions.

The sympathetic increases tension (tone) of the blood vessel walls, making them more resistant to increases in blood pressure; it also has effects on the heart, speeding its action, as well as on the circulation to other organs. It is the sympathetic system which takes over in situations of danger in the well-known 'fight or flight' situation. Activation of this system causes release of adrenalin from the adrenal gland, which then continues to have effects making the organism ready for action.

Stimulating the sympathetic system alters the blood vessel calibre with decrease of blood flow to the skin; this can also be altered by various techniques such as putting the hands in hot water, relaxation, or taking nitroglycerine (a drug used in treatment of angina since it dilates blood vessels and lowers blood pressure, thereby lessening the strain on the heart).

Other factors which control blood vessel diameter are local changes in the concentration of carbon dioxide and acidity, increases of which will cause the blood vessels to dilate. This is important for exercising muscles because, by producing lactic acid as a waste product, they increase the blood supply to the muscles.

Cerebral blood flow

Recent exciting discoveries have revolutionized our ideas of the relationship between thought and blood flow. Previously it was considered that thinking did not use any significant amount of energy and the blood flow to the brain was constant. It is now known, however, that when a group of brain cells is activated it uses up oxygen, produces carbon dioxide, and causes a local increase in blood flow to that area by enlarging the blood vessels.

Using radioactive tracers it is now possible to follow these changes and remarkable pictures have been obtained. For instance, the resting pattern of blood flow shows a marked increase in the frontal areas; talking to the subject causes a decrease of flow to these areas whilst part of the temporal lobe of the brain shows a marked increase of activity—dynamic proof of the long-held hypothesis that this area is one of the speech centres. Similar things happen when other intellectual activities are undertaken so that these techniques confirm localization of various functions in specific areas of the brain.

This close relationship between blood vessels and brain cells leads to interesting possibilities. For instance, if the control of blood vessels were to be deranged, subtle changes in brain function could be expected; this has been confirmed in certain forms of mental disease.

Pain has been shown to increase metabolism in the brain and to dilate vessels generally. The increase in vessel diameter makes small local controlling changes more difficult and this could explain why thinking becomes more difficult during severe pain. The paradox is that pain, like stress, produces increased sympathetic activity, yet it *increases* blood flow to the brain. The resulting vasoconstriction would be expected to decrease it. The answer is probably that the sympathetic controls the larger, so-called resistance vessels, while pain in this context activates local capillaries.

The system which controls blood flow to the brain is highly complex as it is affected by nervous factors, circulating chemicals (amines), and outside factors such as pain, as well as by mental processes. An interesting experiment highlighted the importance of the latter: subjects had to solve problems of mental arithmetic while their brain blood flow was being measured. There was a slight increase to appropriate areas but this became greatly magnified when they were offered money for the successful solution to the problems. This shows that motivation and concentration have a direct effect on the blood flow to the brain and the experiment clearly confirms yet another psychosomatic link.

5

What brings on a migraine attack?

Although a good deal is known about the factors that make blood vessels change their size, it is still uncertain what brings on a migraine attack.

Only a minority of people suffer from migraine but it is quite possible that others would also suffer, given certain circumstances. Even those with the base-line tendency to get attacks vary enormously in their liability to attacks, from sufferers who have almost continual attacks to others who·get them only once in many years.

Just as there are many factors in the tendency to migraine, e.g. age, sex, inheritance, so there are even more in the stimuli that trigger an attack. The list of these trigger factors is large and includes:

Anxiety
Tension
Depression
Shock
Frustration
Hard work

Exercise
Sexual intercourse

Changes in biological rhythm
Changes in sleep pattern

Glare
Weather changes
Cold

Hot baths

Irregular meals
Fasting
Alcohol
Smoking

Certain foods
   cheese
   chocolate
   citrus fruits
   fried foods
   butter

Menstruation
Oral contraceptives
Menopause

High blood pressure
Other facial pains, e.g. toothache
Head colds
Hayfever

Although the number here seems large, it is not by any means inclusive so it is not surprising to hear the claim that 'almost anything can spark off a migraine attack'. For this reason many sufferers find it difficult to pin-point the actual trigger.

Of all the factors invoked, diet and stress are the two commonest.

Diet

Fasting

It is well known that going without food can bring on an attack of migraine. The explanation often given is that, during fasting, the sugar in the blood falls to a low level (hypoglycaemia) and that this provokes an attack. In fact, there are normally body reserves which can be converted to glucose during fasting, so that the blood sugar level does not become dangerously low.

When sugar is eaten, the hormone insulin is released. Its action is to lower the blood sugar level, and it does this in both normal subjects and migraine sufferers, but the low levels last longer than expected in the latter group. Sugar is absorbed in the same way in both sufferers and normals but the release of insulin in response is not quite the same. Using a hormone that releases glucose (glucagon) showed that there was a consistently smaller resultant rise of blood glucose in sufferers than in non-sufferers, and that other abnormalities took longer to return to normal.

In spite of these studies, there is no scientific evidence that sufferers from migraine have a lower level of blood sugar than others. It is probable that it is other changes in the blood associated with fasting which are the trigger factors.

Food headaches

We saw in Chapter 4 that there are chemical substances in certain foods that can cause a headache, e.g. in the Chinese restaurant syndrome (glutamate), the hot-dog headache

39

(nitrites), and other foods that produce headache because of their physical characteristics, e.g. ice-cream headache. These headaches are not usually typically migrainous.

Probably less than 10 per cent of migraine attacks are due to food.

Cheese. There is no doubt that at some stage in their lives certain sufferers repeatedly get migraine after eating cheese. However, at other times they may not. The substance thought to be responsible is tyramine, but giving this to cheese-reactive patients does not always produce a migraine attack. Interestingly enough, it was more likely to do so if, instead of being swallowed, it was fed into a vein.

Chocolate. This is another substance that provokes migraine and also contains tyramine. However, it is now thought that another amine, phenyl ethylamine, is more likely to be responsible.

An experiment was performed on four migrainous sufferers who thought their attacks were brought on by chocolate. Each week they took a capsule and for four months recorded their headaches. All the capsules looked alike but some contained chocolate whilst the others contained a non-active substance (lactose). The 'guinea-pigs', who happened to be doctors, did not know which was which and, at the end of four months, the number of headaches following each type of capsule was found to be the same. This experiment shows how cautious we should be when aportioning blame to trigger factors.

Tea and coffee. One patient suffered repeated severe attacks of migraine, resistant to all forms of treatment. He was found to be highly sensitive to tea and when this was excluded from his diet he improved.

Another sufferer who used to get severe pains had been labelled neurotic but, when given tea or coffee by a tube into her stomach (so that she could not taste it), she developed the pains and her pulse doubled in rate, whilst giving water through the tube had no such effect. After stopping these offending substances she had no further attacks.

The active constituents of tea and coffee include caffeine and theophylline, substances which prevent the breakdown of a high energy compound, cyclic AMP. The build-up of this substance makes the body far more sensitive to the action of the sympathetic nervous system. This type of food allergy is an increased sensitivity of stimulation after taking tea or coffee.

Alcohol. This is the commonest 'food' taken. It is well known for its capacity to widen blood vessels. The 'hangover' headache following excessive intake is well known, but many migraine sufferers are particular sensitive to alcohol, especially red wine and port. This cannot be solely due to the content of pure alcohol but may well be related to other substances (higher esters) which accumulate during long-term storage.

Other foods

Almost every other food has been said to cause migraine, the commoner examples being citrus fruits and meat.

One migraine subject always had an attack of headache some hours after eating pork, but only when tired or under emotional stress, and could eat pork with impunity if in 'good condition'. With skin tests he was found to be sensitive to pork but also many other types of food.

Here we have an illustration of the fact that it is not necessarily a single factor that induces an attack. In addition to the sufferer having the propensity to develop the attack, one single stimulus—in this case, pork—may not be enough but another—in this case, fatigue—had to be present.

Food allergy

'Allergy' is a vague term but when used in its medical sense means an altered reactivity of the body to a stimulus in the

41

environment. Because so many disorders are said to be allergic in origin, scientists are reluctant to accept this explanation unless confirmation is obtained by immunological tests. With migraine this is not often the case, partly because the allergic substance in the food is difficult to isolate.

Stress

Stress is one of the most misused words in the English language, and its precise meaning is often forgotten. It is defined in the *Shorter Oxford Dictionary* as a 'demand upon energy'. This is a difficult concept to apply to the human body and not a factor that can easily be measured. Although breaking a leg is caused by undue stress, it is not this mechanical use of the word that is usually intended; more often, the implication is a strain on the mind (psyche) with a consequent decreased ability to cope. There are some people to whom stress is a challenge to be overcome who are unhappy without tension in their lives; there are others who cannot tolerate any form of stress. Most people fell between the two extremes, their responses depending on the situation. Many studies have been undertaken on stress, particularly in its part in relation to heart disease; based on these studies people have been classified into two groups: 'A' type and 'B' type. The 'A' type takes stress badly, almost as a personal affront, getting tense, edgy, 'rushing about', and exhibiting a high degree of tension; the 'B' type is much more relaxed and, when under stress, tends to utilize the situation in a constructive manner. It is found that type 'A' is almost twice as likely to develop heart attacks as type 'B'. Comparable studies have not yet been done in migraine but personality does seem to play a large part in determining who gets migraine, and it may well be that different responses to stress are important in determining the frequency of attacks.

It is not known whether stress provokes migraine by increasing the production of adrenaline or noradrenaline or whether its effect is unrelated to biochemical changes.

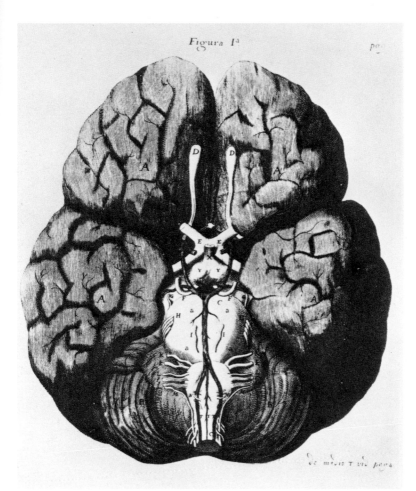

PLATE 1. The original drawing by Sir Christopher Wren (the architect of St. Paul's Cathedral) of the circle of Willis (the arteries of the base of the brain).

D — olfactory nerves (for smell)

E — the optic chiasm (for vision)

F — the two posterior cerebral arteries arise near here from the single basilar artery which has been formed by junction of the two vertebral arteries (bottom of the drawing).

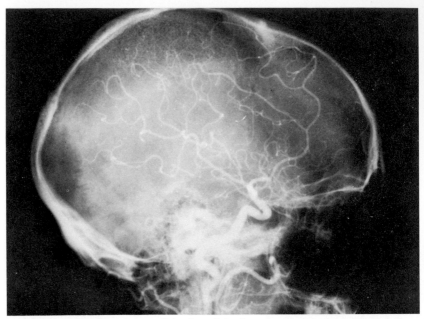

PLATE 2. A carotid arteriogram (injection of dye into the carotid artery) showing the branches within the head.

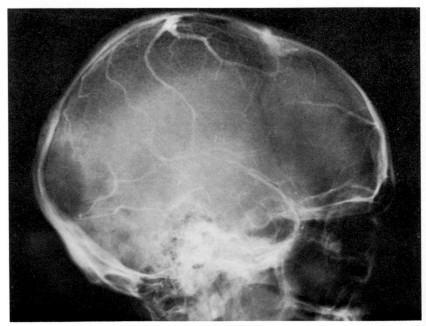

PLATE 3. The late phase of the arteriogram showing the veins of the brain.

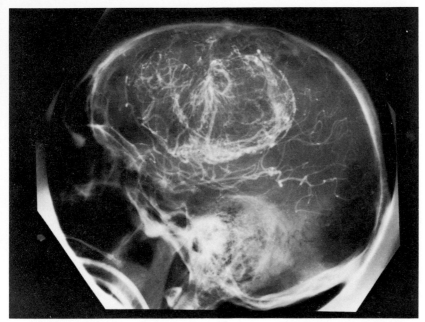

PLATE 4. An arteriogram showing a brain tumour fed by numerous extra blood vessels.

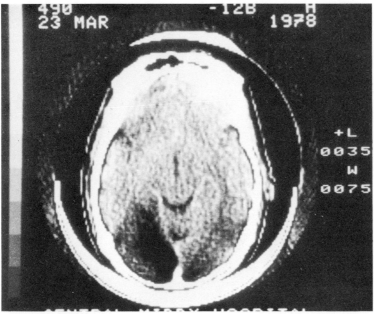

PLATE 5. Computerized tomographic (CT) scan of a patient who developed a stroke after a severe migraine attack. The scan shows a horizontal section through the head and reveals a damaged area of brain (dark oval shape at the bottom left hand corner).

What brings on a migraine attack?

Exercise

Exercise can provoke attacks of migraine but it has also been recommended as a prevention of attacks. The truth is that exercise is a particular form of stress, so that the same chemical changes take place, e.g. an outpouring of adrenal hormones which makes the heart beat faster to supply more blood to the exercising muscles.

Menstrual migraine

Many women sufferers often relate their migraine attacks to the menstrual cycle. If the week before is considered pre-menstrual and the week after post-menstrual, then three of the four weeks of the cycle could be thought of as closely related to menstruation, and it is not surprising that the majority of attacks should occur during that period. However, the action of the female hormones (oestrogen and progesterone) on blood vessels in the lining of the womb during the menstrual cycle is of great relevance to migraine. The uterine blood vessels become elongated, twisted, and thick-walled, and similar changes occur elsewhere in the body. If the level of progesterone drops suddenly, bleeding occurs from the womb, and headaches are more frequent. This is the pattern of pre-menstrual migraine and it is for this reason that progesterone supplements have been given for the prevention of migraine attacks at this time.

Some women have headaches a week before their period; others have them on the first day or during the last days of their period; yet others get them at the time of ovulation i.e. midway between the menstrual periods.

Before the menstrual period, women often complain of increased weight due to water retention. This, too, has been associated with migraine attacks and, not infrequently, the disappearance of the attack is marked by an excessive excretion of urine.

Headaches may become more frequent and troublesome

43

at puberty, and this also is probably related to hormonal changes. In adult life, there is a tendency for headaches to get better with increasing age, but this is not consistent and some women may get a worsening of the headache about the time of the menopause. Eighty per cent of women who suffer from headaches lose them during pregnancy although, in some, headaches may become worse in the early stages.

'The pill'

Progesterone, given in the first half of the cycle, prevents ovulation and is the basis for oral contraceptives.

Headaches often come on soon after starting the first course of the contraceptive pill. Rarely they can be very severe and accompanied by signs of malfunction of the nervous system such as the temporary loss of use of a limb or transient blindness, presumably due to a drop in blood flow to the appropriate part of the brain. These symptoms must always be taken seriously.

Some women taking the pill become severely depressed; this is of interest in the light of the relationship of migraine and depression.

Analysis of sufferers attending Migraine Clinics suggest that taking oral contraceptives is a major factor among those who come during an acute attack of migraine; this finding supports the hypothesis that oral contraceptives alter the threshold to migraine making people taking them more susceptible to attacks. On the other hand in some women, migraine attacks cease soon after they start to take the pill.

How is the headache caused?

Although there are many trigger factors that set off an attack of migraine, the precise way in which this is done is still uncertain. It is known that a change in the diameter (calibre) of vessels to the head play a part; this alteration can be due to nervous or chemical changes.

What brings on a migraine attack?

The passage of an impulse down a nerve is electrical, in other words, there is a wave of changing charge moving down the nerve fibre. On the other hand, the passage of impulses from nerve to nerve is purely chemical, as is the passage of the nerve impulse to the muscle which the nerve controls. Chemicals are stored in the end-buttons of the nerve and, with the arrival of the impulse, packets of these are released either into the space between nerves, where they lead to a further nervous impulse, or into the space between nerve and muscle to cause muscle contraction. In the gap between the nerve terminal and its target are enzymes (specific chemicals that catalyse, or speed up, chemical reactions); these help destroy any transmitter substances not used, or which do not find their way back to their site of origin. An example of one of these enzymes is monoamine oxidase, or MAO.

Nervous transmitters

There are three main types of substances acting as nervous transmitters: acetylcholine, catecholamines, and peptides. *Acetylcholine* is the prime transmitter for the parasympathetic nervous system, which with the sympathetic system makes up the autonomic nervous system. Its effects are to some extent opposite to those of the sympathetic nerves: the heart is slowed, the gut becomes sluggish, the pupils become constricted. Physical exercise can make the effects of the parasympathetic more marked; this is the reason why an athlete often has a slow pulse rate, slow pumping of the heart being more efficient than rapid beating. Acetycholine also controls the muscles of the body, being released at nerve endings in muscle cells (the South American arrow poison, curare, works by blocking the effects of acetylcholine to produce paralysis).

Catecholamines: the sympathetic nervous system uses noradrenalin as a transmitter; this substance can be measured in the blood and its level is raised in situations such as stress or exercise when too much is released to be destroyed or taken up again. Tyramine, mentioned previously as a cause of migraine, has effects similar to those of noradrenalin; β-phenylethylamine is another amino acid invoked in dietary migraine, particularly chocolate; it probably plays a role in transmission of impulse, but its importance is still uncertain. Another catecholamine, serotonin (5-hydroxytryptamine) has marked effects on the brain and is also present in the small blood cells (platelets) concerned in the first stages of blood clotting. Its relevance in the study of migraine is that it has a marked constrictive effect on blood vessels and its release from platelets can cause spasm in the related area.

Apart from their effects on blood vessels as nervous transmitters, amines also have local effects when coming into direct contact with the vessel wall. Cheese and red wine contain tyramine whereas chocolate contains phenylethylamine; once consumed these substances enter the blood stream and exert their effects on blood vessels. In those taking certain drugs for depression they may cause catastrophic rises in blood pressure. The chain reaction in patients on these drugs in no way resembles a migraine attack, however, and is more in keeping with the severe headache found with high blood pressure (hypertensive encephalopathy).

The finding that certain amines can cause vasomotor changes, raising the blood pressure and producing severe headaches, is of interest in the study of the causation of vascular headaches.

When small, measured quantities of the catecholamine transmitter tyramine are given, small, reproduceable rises in blood pressure are produced. Migraine patients need less tyramine than other people to achieve the same rise in blood pressure (there is a similar increased sensitivity to tyramine in depressed patients). The explanation may be that there is an increased sensitivity to tyramine in migraine subjects, but it is uncertain whether this is secondary to the headaches or a sensitivity which is always present in migraine patients.

What brings on a migraine attack?

Tyramine raises blood pressure partly by stimulating the release of noradrenaline from nerve endings. These effects could spark off the changes discussed but the most obvious interpretation may not be the actual explanation. When migraine sufferers are given a tablet of tyramine, its metabolism and excretion resembles the results in similar experiments with depressed patients. It would be easy to deduce that migraine is linked to depression biochemically; but all that can be said at present is that certain people who have migraine and others who are depressed are similar in one particular biochemical measurement.

Platelets in migraine

During a migraine attack, the lessening of blood flow may not be entirely due to narrowing of the blood vessels since the blood itself may become more sticky and liable to sludge. Platelets are constituents of blood that have the ability to stick together and form clumps, an essential first stage in the familiar clotting reaction which plugs the gap in a cut vessel and stops bleeding. Occasionally these clumps can produce disease, as in certain forms of stroke, when they pass through the circulation to the brain and cause loss of function. This is not to say that an attack of migraine is like a stroke, but there are certain similarities as far as platelets are concerned.

The platelets of migraine sufferers clump together more easily than those of other people. But since many factors can alter platelet aggregation, this finding might be a secondary effect of the migraine attack. It is possible to measure the aggregation of platelets, either by the response to certain chemicals or by measuring the proportion of clumped platelets in a blood sample. Both these techniques have been used in migraine patients and it was found that some patients have an increased number of clumped platelets; this is present all the time but becomes worse during a migraine attack. This suggests that platelets in migraine subjects are on 'red alert', awaiting only the slightest stimulus to clump together. This abnormality has also been found in relatives of migraine sufferers. Research is now being directed at the alteration of platelet function in the hope that this might eventually be used to prevent migraine attacks.

What makes platelets clump together? Various chemicals can do this, for example substances such as collagen found within blood vessel walls, and vaso-active amines such as adrenalin, noradrenalin, histamine, and serotonin (5HT). But the most potent platelet aggregators are substances called prostaglandins. Discovered about 15 years .ago, they have marked effects on blood vessels and smooth muscle as well as participating in the inflammatory reaction. One of their actions is involved in the contraction of the uterus during labour. Until recently, only the stable members of this family could be studied, but a substance has just been found which lasts only about half a minute and which has a powerful effect on platelets. It is produced by platelets themselves and, when platelets stick together, a sort of cascade process occurs, each platelet producing more of this substance.

Interestingly, the vessel wall itself produces a substance with the opposite effect. This substance, prostacyclin or PGX, in addition to preventing platelets from aggregating, also has a marked action on vessel walls, causing them to dilate. These findings are exciting in their potential but are too recent to have been fully studied in connection with migraine.

When platelets clump together, they produce serotonin, or 5-hydroxytryptamine (5HT), which has a marked constricting effect on blood vessels. During attacks of migraine the amount of 5HT in the platelet clump decreases, while the excretion of the breakdown products of 5HT increases. Experiments suggest that under certain circumstances, 5HT can cause both dilatation of the extracranial carotid artery and constriction of the intracranial carotid artery.

Another interesting finding is that the activity of one form of the enzyme monoamine oxidase (MAO), the function of which is to destroy amines such as serotonin in platelets, is lower during an attack of migraine than at other times. It might be thought that this lowering of MAO activity would lay the body open to amines which would then exert their noxious influence, but this is not so. However, we do not know precisely when this lowering occurs; whether it is a primary change or secondary to the headache; nor do we know what the other MAOs are doing.

This yo-yo behaviour of the platelet MAO in migraine seems to be at odds with findings that people with a consistently low level of platelet MAO are at greater risk of mental illness; a measurement that is constant, highly reproducible, and probably a genetic trait.

In our own studies, we found three individuals who not only had a low level of MAO during a migraine attack but also between attacks. There were no obvious psychiatric problems in any of them but, interestingly, they showed a response to tyramine similar to that found in depression. Although infusions of adrenalin and noradrenalin, as well as hard exercise, seem to increase the activity of MAO, no clear overall picture has emerged as yet.

The responses to all these tests in migraine patients differ from the normal but this does not mean that migraine sufferers are inherently different from other people. It is more likely that there is a gradation from normals to headache sufferers to migraine sufferers. It is because of this lack of sharp distinction that research on migraine is so difficult.

There are certain more clear-cut differences between the migraine sufferer and others. First, migraine can be inherited; second, there is an increased incidence of epilepsy in migraine sufferers, and, third, the EEG (see Chapter 6) may be more often abnormal. The last two differences could be explained by repeated migraine attacks or by drugs used in treatment, and a good deal of research has been done to clarify this particular problem.

6

The investigation of headaches

People with headaches are not only concerned with seeking relief, but are often worried that their headaches may mean something more serious, such as a brain tumour.

Although nearly everyone at some time has a headache, it is only when the headaches become severe or frequent and interfere with daily living that a doctor's advice is sought. Migraine affects approximately one in five people, but only a small percentage of these go to their doctor. How does the doctor decide whether a headache is due to migraine or to another cause and when would he refer a case to a specialist?

History

The most important aspect of a consultation with the doctor is the taking of a history. With headaches as the chief complaint, the doctor asks about the type of headache, its duration and frequency, site, aggravating and relieving factors, accompanying symptoms such as nausea or visual disturbance, as well as the family history and information about previous illnesses. In most cases a definite diagnosis can be made at this stage and the physical examination and special investigations will merely confirm the diagnosis.

Physical examination

The physical examination can include a general examination of all the body's systems, e.g. the pulse is taken, the heart listened to, blood pressure measured, and the abdomen felt.

In a full neurological examination, the cranial nerves are tested one by one. The ability to smell may need to be tested. It is important to test vision, especially visual acuity and visual fields. The ophthalmoscope is an instrument designed so that the doctor can look at the optic nerve and the blood vessels at the back of the retina; its use is particularly important in certain cases. Movements of the eye, facial muscles, soft palate, and shoulder movements are tested as are sensation on the face and hearing.

The power of the muscles and sensation in the rest of the body is then tested as are fine movements and co-ordination. The reflexes are tapped to see if they are equally brisk on each side and the sole of the foot scratched: a down-going toe in response to this is normal. At some stage the doctor will listen over the neck, head, and eyes for any murmurs, noises caused by turbulence in blood flow produced by narrowings or malformations in blood vessels.

In most cases of headache, the examination is negative, suggesting that all is well but, occasionally, a small change may alert the doctor to the possibility of a more serious problem and it is then that the patient may be referred to the specialist for investigations.

Special investigations

In the present scientific era, there is a tendency to rely too much on machines, requests being made for every possible test in the hope that something will show up. This is not only wasteful but the results, instead of being reassuring, can be grossly misleading. Statistically, the more tests that are done, the greater the number of abnormal results. This produces a vicious circle where a healthy patient is investigated extensively to explain a chemical abnormality at great expense; the abnormal results could well be fortuitous or valueless in the first place.

With preparatory thought, these disadvantages could be avoided. The purpose of special investigations is to provide information beyond that given by the history and clinical examination so that it is important to define the questions which it is hoped the investigations will answer. The tests most useful in the diagnosis of a headache can be divided, for convenience, into those on the blood and others.

Blood tests

When a sample of blood is analysed, information is obtained about the state of the blood cells and the fluid (serum) in which they float.

Blood cells. The main cell in the blood is the red blood corpuscle which contains a chemical that carries oxygen (haemoglobin). Anaemia occurs when the level of haemoglobin drops but, in certain circumstances, there can be too much haemoglobin so that the blood becomes thicker and passes through the small vessels less readily, and this may cause migranous symptoms.

Another important test is to examine the rate at which red blood cells settle when put in a vertical glass tube. This is called the erythrocyte sedimentation rate (e.s.r.). In a patient with headache due to sinusitis or temporal arteritis (see Chapter 2), the rate of sedimentation will be rapid and produce a high e.s.r.

Another important type of cell is the white blood corpuscle which helps ward off infection. These can fairly easily be counted and when the count is too low this means there is either an abnormality in production, or they are being destroyed too rapidly. During many types of infection, there is a high count and, as there are several varieties of white blood corpuscle, the group that is increased indicates the type of infection. This estimation may be of value, for example, in distinguishing a migraine attack, where the white cell count will be normal, from sinusitis, where the count will be high.

Tests can also be done on platelets to see how easily they clump together (aggregate). This is done by separating the platelets from the rest of the blood and putting them in a chamber through which a beam of light is shone; a substance which aggregates platelets is added to the platelet suspension so that the transmission of the beam of light through the chamber becomes stronger. Some migraine patients have platelets which are particularly prone to aggregate (see Chapter 5).

The serum

In patients with rarer types of headache it may be necessary to perform tests on the serum, which is obtained by spinning blood in a centrifuge to separate off the cells. In certain allergic illnesses which can cause headache, antibodies to foreign substances can be estimated.

Other special investigations

X-rays. The skull X-ray gives only limited information, e.g. it will show fractures, sinusitis, or inflammation of the bone. A tumour within the skull may show itself by thinning or thickening of the bone overlying it. Shadows of calcium can be seen in various areas within the skull cavity, e.g. a common place is the pineal gland; this is normal but, since this gland is central, a displacement signifies a growth pushing it to the other side. Calcium can also be seen when deposited in a slow-growing tumour, abscess, or blood vessel malformation. These alarming features are virtually never found in a patient with migraine. In fact, the skull X-ray of 100 people without headaches would show abnormalities about as often as those of 100 migraine sufferers. The X-ray is justified on the grounds that something may be discovered, albeit rarely.

An X-ray of the chest is occasionally done as a screening measure in eliminating certain causes of headache, e.g. in tumour of the lung, which may spread to the head.

Since headache may be due to neck trouble, an X-ray of the cervical spine is sometimes indicated. Although migraine is not usually caused by problems in the neck, wear and tear of the neck vertebrae can cause pain with consequent spasm of the neck muscles, which pull on the scalp to give tension (muscle contraction) headache; treatment of arthritic pain can often relieve these headaches. Pressure on the roots of the cervical nerves also causes pain, particularly over the back of the head.

Electroencephalography (EEG). Brain cells produce minute fluctuations in electric current which can be recorded by placing on various parts of the head small metal discs attached to suitable amplifiers.

The numerous electrical impulses which are associated with the living brain tend to produce a particular repetitive pattern. With the eyes closed, *alpha* rhythm appears, i.e. a rhythm consisting of waves lasting one-tenth of a second; with the eyes opened so that the brain is alerted, this rhythm disappears. Faster rhythms may be seen when the patient is on tranquillizers, and slower (theta) rhythms indicate malfunctions or tumours of the brain.

These slower rhythms are also seen in some patients with migraine, particularly during an attack, when they may indicate a transient decrease in circulation. Most patients with migraine have a normal EEG but the abnormalities found consist mainly of slow wave activity, more often over only one temporal lobe. EEG findings are not always conclusive since many different abnormalities can give identical EEG changes. A small percentage of 'normal' people without symptoms have EEG 'abnormalities' but these occur more commonly in migraine patients and become more pronounced during an attack. The EEG can therefore be a help both in assessing the severity of attacks and in excluding diagnoses other than migraine; patients with hemiplegic migraine particularly tend to have severe persisting EEG abnormalities on the relevant side of the head.

During one stage of the EEG examination, the patient is asked to 'overbreathe', i.e. to breathe rapidly and deeply; this causes carbon dioxide to be 'blown off' producing a change in the acidity of the blood. Overbreathing can bring out latent abnormalities and, although migraine patients have slightly different responses to overbreathing, the meaning of this is uncertain. It may be that they are more anxious as a group with a greater tendency to overbreathing, i.e. an anxiety response. A more likely explanation is that their blood vessels are unduly sensitive to changes in blood acidity.

Another EEG technique to reveal latent abnormalities is the response to a *stroboscope*, a machine that produces flashing lights (flicker) at different frequencies. In the vast majority of migraine subjects, these responses are made to a much greater range of flash frequencies than in normal subjects but, as a similar phenomenon was observed in people with anxiety and tension who do not suffer from migraine, its significance is uncertain. The EEG changes found in migraine may be very similar to those found in epilepsy, and on the basis of the EEG records it would be difficult to distinguish between the two conditions.

The EEG can indicate a structural abnormality but it is not always possible to distinguish one cause of structural abnormality from another; indeed, some deep-seated lesions may cause no EEG abnormality or only minimal generalized changes.

The answer to the question of what the EEG does is that it supplies a useful piece of the jigsaw puzzle but rarely gives the whole answer to a diagnostic problem on its own. Rather like the skull X-ray, the EEG will reveal something unsuspected only in some instances, when more extensive investigations are indicated.

Visual evoked potentials. The visual evoked response is a more recent technique that is also based on recording electrical activity from the brain. It is still only a research tool as far as migraine is concerned. When an object is seen, an electrical discharge passes along the optic pathway to cause a specific but tiny response in the brain. When the same impulse is presented repeatedly the responses can be added up by an EEG machine to give a much bigger response, shown on a screen as a wave-form. Using this technique, the time taken for the impulse to travel along the optic pathways can be measured, by taking the time from seeing the object (the stimulus) to the peak of the wave. Diseases such as inflammation or pressure on the optic nerve will slow the response, whilst damage to the brain can alter the shape of the wave-form.

Because it has been suggested that repeated attacks of severe migraine could possibly damage the brain, VERs have been done in some cases for the purposes of research. Patients with migraine had VERs measured from each side of the head. Migraine patients have a delay in the time interval from the stimulus to the wave, indicating that the nerve impulse travels more slowly through the brain than in non-migrainous subjects. The wave responses, rather than being smaller, were in fact larger, and this did not seem to make sense nor be easily explicable. Those whose headaches were on the left side of the head had a much bigger wave-form than those whose headaches were on both sides or on the right side, another observation for which there is as yet no certain explanation.

The prolonged latency can be explained more easily: this is *not* due to stroke-like damage since in strokes the latencies are normal (only the height of the waves is less). In certain situations changing the neurotransmitters in the brain can alter the latency, so the most likely explanation is that migraine patients have some difference with respect to neurotransmitters. Which neurotransmitter is involved is not yet known, but it is unlikely to be due to noradrenalin or adrenalin since stress can actually speed up the response.

These differences between migraine subjects and non-sufferers are still circumstantial and to a large extent contradictory, suggesting again that migraine is possibly not a single disorder.

Brain scanning. In certain cases of headache, a brain scan, of which there are two types, may need to be done. One type relies on the uptake of a radioactive isotope by abnormal tissue, such as a tumour. The patient is given an injection of a short-lived radioactive isotope into an arm vein from where it enters the arterial system and goes through the brain, ascending via the carotid arteries. By using a camera the isotope is followed up the carotid arteries to each cerebral hemisphere, where the radioactivity is then 'washed out'. The flow of the isotope through the brain helps to distinguish between a tumour, which has a relatively high flow, and a stroke in which case the flow is very low. It is a quick and easy test to do but is not available in every hospital.

The other type of scanning is also quick and easy but is even less readily available, although it has revolutionized diagnosis. Computerized axial tomographic (CT or CAT) scanning examines 'slices' of brain by moving the X-ray machine in such a way that the slice is motionless relative to the areas in front of, and behind, it. The moving areas become blurred while the 'slice' – the area to be examined – retains its sharpness and is defined more clearly. The CT technique depends on the fact that different tissues absorb different amounts of radiation so that it is then easy to identify the different structures to see if there is any abnormality. Its precise place in migraine is still controversial but some reports suggest that in very severe cases there may be evidence of persistent brain changes (Plate 5).

These investigations carry no risk and are performed without fear of complication. Rarely, other X-ray techniques, which rely on the introduction of substances opaque to X-ray into either blood vessels (arteriography) or the subarachnoid space (air encephalography), have to be done in order to define the structures more clearly on X-ray films. These tests are often done under a general anaesthetic (see Plate 4).

Arteriography and air encephalography. These investigations reveal a good deal because the size and shape of the blood vessels can be seen. This is not only important with someone at risk from a stroke, when a blockage or narrowing of an artery can be revealed and treated, but also because other abnormalities of the vessels can be seen, for example, a balloonlike distension (aneurysm) found at the junction of two vessels making up the circle of Willis (see Plate 1). This can cause headache as well as pressure on sensitive structures leading to paralysis of one of the cranial nerves. Small leaks from such an aneurysm, or tiny expansions of it, can cause headaches resembling migraine. If it bursts, the consequent haemorrhage can be catastrophic.

Another abnormality is a growth of blood vessels rather like the strawberry birthmark seen on the skin. These are called arteriovenous malformations and vary in size; their presence will be suspected if the doctor hears a murmur, the noise of turbulent blood. These malformations cause a number of symptoms; e.g. epilepsy or haemorrhage. They may occasionally cause weakness of one side of the body, and can also be associated with a migraine-like syndrome, as in the following case:

A 24-year-old man came to the migraine clinic complaining of headache over the right side of his head associated with usual symptoms of classical migraine. Careful examination revealed no abnormality and skull X-rays, EEG, and isotope brain scan were all normal. The condition was treated as migraine and the patient responded well. Within a few weeks he collapsed at work having had a subarachnoid haemorrhage. Arteriography revealed a small arteriovenous malformation in the front part of the brain. He was operated on, the malformation successfully removed and he suffered no further headaches.

The cerebrospinal fluid is produced in spaces within the brain (the ventricles) and circulates through to the surface of the brain where it bathes the brain and spinal cord and is then re-absorbed. Air encephalography is performed by replacing the cerebrospinal fluid obtained by lumbar puncture with air. The air bubble enters the ventricles and, being of a different density to brain and cerebrospinal fluid, is seen as a dark area on the X-ray; any abnormalities in brain structure will be clearly shown.

Following encephalography the patient must lie flat for a day to prevent the development of headache which is caused by traction on the dura as the brain sags slightly because of low pressure of the cerebrospinal fluid. (A similar headache may be experienced when the patient is dehydrated, or as part of the 'hangover' following excessive alcohol intake.)

7

Treatment without drugs

There is no drug, not even aspirin, that does not have side-effects. It has been estimated that nearly one-third of all illnesses are iatrogenic, i.e. due to drugs. For this reason, most sufferers would prefer to do without drugs if possible.

There are two main approaches to therapy: first, prevention and, second, treatment of the symptoms as soon as they occur. The majority of sufferers from migraine do not go to their doctor and will only do so if the frequency of the headaches suddenly increases. This increase may be due either to an alteration in life circumstances, e.g. increasing stress, or increased exposure to particular precipitants. There may also be a combination of the two, for example, when someone whose headaches are made worse by tobacco smokes more under stress; the combination of these two factors, smoking and stress, is likely to aggravate migraine more than either one singly.

The placebo response

The word placebo means 'I will please'. It is used to describe a response found with many illnesses including, surprisingly, serious ones, namely the tendency of the patient to get better on treatment which theoretically should have no effect at all. Because the patient *believes* that the treatment is helping, he *is* helped because symptoms disappear; indeed occasionally 'physical' (organic) lesions have been known to diminish, showing the close relationship between the mind and body. Some types of faith-healing probably work in this way, fortifying the patient, boosting confidence that something is being done, and increasing the body's recuperative powers. There is no doubt that the psychological status of a person affects many of the body's mechanisms.

Migraine

The placebo response is influenced to a great extent by the attitudes and personality of the attending therapist, and this is illustrated by the two following cases:

A 30-year-old housewife had headaches of increasing frequency and intensity. Her 4½-year-old daughter was suffering from feeding problems and the woman was becoming increasingly frustrated and angry so that at times she assaulted the child physically. During her first clinic visit the woman confessed her problems to a friendly and sympathetic physician and, by the end of the interview, was much relieved. A remission from headaches of several weeks followed. At her next visit the physician adopted a stern and critical attitude and, ten minutes later, she began to have a severe migraine which responded to the injection of ergotamine.

A 44-year-old woman had frequent migraine attacks. She was given a box of placebo pills with words of kindness, reassurance, and indications of extreme interest. It was also emphasized that she had no serious structural defect or tumour, and she left the clinic feeling relaxed and secure. For six weeks following the interview she was headache-free, but gradually the condition began to creep back.

This last case history exemplifies a characteristic of migraine. It is quite common for a migraine sufferer to respond very well initially to any new therapeutic regime, but it is nearly as common for the headaches to return subsequently as badly as ever. The explanation is that the initial placebo response wears off and indicates that the treatment has had no specific effect of its own. Another interesting feature is the amazing variety of totally different drugs which seem to be effective in the treatment of migraine. It is for this reason that claims of success for a particular form of treatment have to be carefully analysed. The more attention and interest a patient gets, the greater the placebo effect will be. To some extent this may explain the good effect of certain dietary treatment or, indeed, any treatment in which the patient obtains a good deal of attention.

Avoidance of stress

Stress can undoubtedly act as a provocative factor in many

patients and a logical form of treatment is to lessen this, if possible.

Frustrating situations are met with in nearly all walks of life. One patient told his story as follows:

From the standpoint of migraine, the year beginning 1 July was note-worthy because of the infrequency and mildness of attacks; during this period the amount of work in which I had been engaged just filled each day, making it possible to maintain certain personal ideals of perfec-tion. Since November the greatest amount of concentration has been directed to quantitative determinations in a large number of microscopic sections of tissues. Frequent short periods of this rather monotonous work during almost every day had not been unpleasant. On 4 February it was suggested that an attempt be made to complete this research suf-ficiently to present an abstract of the work to a scientific society within 16 days for consideration as a presentation at a later date. Accepting this suggestion I therefore increased my concentration on this problem by working in the evenings. It soon became evident that the amount of work accomplished was falling far short of any schedule that would produce a sufficient number of figures within this time, and furthermore, the work was for the first time becoming distasteful. In the night, after the second evening in the laboratory I was awakened by an ache over the right eye associated with nausea. After a period of semi-wakefulness, sleep was resumed and the next day the only trace of a headache was pain on the right side of the head on coughing. After the third evening of laboratory work I was awakened at 4 a.m. by an ache over the left eye associated with nausea. Unlike the symptoms of the previous night they rapidly increased in severity until it became necessary to get in a hot bath to secure some relief. When I returned to bed, the pain and nausea resumed their former severity and 1 gram of codeine finally relieved their symptoms and allowed a few hours of sleep. During the entire next day there were nausea and a constant severe generalized headache extending downward into the back of the neck, which was made worse by walking, talking or reaching. The following morning the symptoms had vanished.

This story will strike a chord with almost every migraine sufferer. Although it is possible to explain this sort of tension on a biochemical basis, too few studies have been done in chronic stress situations to pinpoint the problem but the existence of two different personality types is pertinent. Type 'B' people who thrive on challenges get a 'charge or kick' by being active and doing things and may in fact be

61

depressed and lethargic when under-stimulated; with this personality, absence of stress may spark off headaches. The patient above is an example of a Type 'A' personality, who reacted badly to stress.

Although a certain amount of stress is a normal part of human existence, excessive amounts can undoubtedly act as a provocative factor. In many patients it therefore seems logical to try to lessen this, if possible. The first step, which often helps greatly, is to remove any worries regarding the nature of migraine with an explanation as well as reassurance that there is nothing more seriously wrong. Only very rarely are worries about the nature of the illness sufficiently intractable to need referral to a psychiatrist.

Although life-style cannot always be changed, the worsening of any stress disease indicates the need for its re-examination. Obvious examples include the person in business or one of the professions who never takes time off to relax; here the important point to emphasize is that one headache a month equals one day lost from work a month, so that it is a good investment to take some time off. The type 'A' person may find periods of relaxation which take the form of just staring at the ceiling punitive; in this sort of case, physical exercise may be indicated, starting gently in those unaccustomed to it.

Although it is impractical to suggest that the hard-working businessman gives up his job, it is possible to help him cope with the pressures involved in his work. By preventing the physiological (e.g. hormonal) changes caused by stress, the cycle of chemical changes involved in migraine can be arrested. One useful method of achieving this is relaxation therapy where many of the changes induced are the reverse of those seen in the tension headache/migraine syndrome. During relaxation certain psyiological changes occur, e.g. muscle tone is decreased, and respiration and the heart rate slow; all of these are manifestations of a decrease in the tone of sympathetic muscles. Historically, there have been numerous types of relaxation therapy: the Japanese communal bath, which is not used for cleansing purposes, the Finnish sauna,

Treatment without drugs

the American 'whirlpool', and massage are all attempts in this direction. There is some evidence that teaching a tense person to relax is of benefit in reducing the incidence of headaches but it is difficult to separate this improvement from the placebo response, so that the claims to success of relaxation therapy are difficult to interpret.

Often those persons who most need relaxation find the greatest difficulty in obtaining it. One way recommended for assessing a person's state of tension is to imitate his posture, e.g. sitting on the edge of the chair leaning forward with shoulders hunched and fists clenched. If the patient holds this posture for a few minutes, there will be a feeling of discomfort. If, on breathing out rapidly there is a smooth exhalation, relaxation is possible but interrupted breathing with an involuntary holding of the breath implies that the patient may be resistant to relaxation therapy.

Relaxation therapy aims at providing a variety of positive steps to ensure that the last remains of tension have been removed. Relaxation is much easier in a warm quiet room. Many hospitals and therapists have their own techniques for relaxation and the summary of such a method given in the appendix to this book is typical of many currently available.

Weekend migraine

In many cases, there is a tendency for migraine to occur at weekends, on the first day of a holiday, or when a social engagement is planned. Because of these 'relaxation' or 'let-down' headaches, these sufferers feel robbed of their pleasures. This sort of headache may be due to biological readjustments in those who are in a sense addicted to activity, i.e. 'workaholics'; it is possible that biochemical changes caused by cessation of activity could be the trigger factor.

Psychiatric treatment

Many patients with migraine have some degree of depression

but this may be secondary to their headaches rather than a primary cause. In these cases, the opinion of a psychiatrist is of great value since their training facilitates assessment of which patient will respond best to a particular method of therapy. Some experts favour a more complex interpretation of headaches based on psychoanalytic theory but this approach has not often proved helpful.

Biofeedback

Biofeedback is the term used for the methods by which conscious control can be gained of functions that are usually automatic. This is achieved by 'feeding back' to the patient information about the automatic function so that its control can be modified. Possibly the commonest use of biofeedback is in the control of blood pressure, where patients are told to concentrate in various ways and the results of their efforts are relayed to them; most people can learn a technique which will reduce their blood pressure, an effect which can be maintained. Epileptic patients often say 'I almost had an attack but I felt it coming and fought it off'—an interpretation of events verified using EEG monitoring; patients can be taught to suppress epileptic activity when the EEG information is fed back to them but the mechanism of this suppression is unknown.

There have been many attempts to treat migraine in the same way. Three types of information can be relayed to the migraine sufferer, the first of which is the degree of distension of the temporal artery. During an attack of migraine, the temporal artery becomes dilated and it is possible for sufferers to learn to reduce the diameter of the temporal artery, and so abort attacks.

Muscle contraction can also be brought under feedback control. When a patient develops a migraine associated with neck muscle tension, contraction of the neck can be recorded using a machine—the electromyograph (EMG). Therapy consists of feeding back to the patient information on the amount of muscle activity in the neck, so encouraging him to relax. Results have been fairly encouraging but there is a great placebo effect; the relief of tension can work by affecting the stress provoking the migraine attack, and other forms of relaxation not using biofeedback can also relieve the tension in the muscles of the neck.

Thirdly, there is an increase in temperature over the head during a migraine attack with an increase in blood flow; this is most marked during an attack of cluster headache. The response of blood vessels of the limbs to increased blood flow is abnormal in migraine sufferers, and increasing the blood flow through the skin of the hand is associated with a decreased flow of blood to the skin of the forehead. People can alter the blood flow through their hands following appropriate concentration using biofeedback and, interestingly enough, it is the dominant hand which shows the best response. Using biofeedback, the patient can be trained to warm his hand when an attack is coming on. This technique is not effective in all sufferers, however, because the responses of the blood vessels vary. (Similar responses to the same stimuli occur in anger: some people go white due to constriction of their blood vessels whilst others go red, due to dilation of their blood vessels.)

Hand-warming is worth trying as the biofeedback apparatus required is fairly simple, and consists of a surface thermometer attached to the hand with a means of relaying the information to the patient; these devices are becoming available commercially and are not too expensive. The patient sits in a relaxed position and attempts various thoughts in order to obtain vessel constriction until a satisfactory lessening in blood flow is obtained, as evidenced by a small decrease in temperature. It is the *skin* temperature that is important so there is no point in clenching the hand. With practice, when the technique has been mastered, changes in temperature of one to two degrees can be achieved.

Anecdotal reports bear out the usefulness of the method: one patient, who suffered from severe cluster headaches, spontaneously said 'I know it sounds funny, but I think that if I concentrate I can make my hand feel warmer and then the pain in my head seems to get better.'

Meditation

The many different forms of meditation can be grouped into two general categories: those concerned with 'emptying the mind' and those in which internal thoughts are built up and maintained by an effort of concentration.

Transcendental meditation became very fashionable in the West during the 1960s and much is claimed for it by headache sufferers. It is not surprising that an act of relaxation or withdrawal from everyday activities is associated with relief of tension which produces a reduction in headache frequency. It is less likely to be effective once a headache has started, presumably because the metabolic changes which occur during the headache make it difficult to maintain the appropriate state of mind.

Yoga

Yoga is an ancient Indian technique of achieving total bodily and mental control in an attempt to reach new heights of awareness and in promoting relaxation. There have been several trials of yoga methods of meditation in the prevention of migraine and the results, although preliminary, are encouraging.

'Yoga of the body' is concerned with making the body a fit vehicle for the mind as it meditates. The first precepts of control are based on the type of foods ingested, and is similar to much of the dietary advice often given for migraine: no citrus fruits, little cheese, no alcohol or wine, no garlic or onions and, in addition, no smoking. Garlic and onions are excluded because they may cause gastric upset. Meals are taken three times a day, the stomach being 'half filled with food, a quarter filled with water and one quarter left empty', to avoid any feeling of fullness. Food has to be chewed thoroughly and eaten slowly (in contrast to the gulping of quick snack lunches seen in British pubs). Constipation is avoided by adding bran to the diet. Much of this advice is commonsense and it is understandable that, with this regime, the body will function in a better way.

The exercises of yoga are divided into those in which breathing is the main concern, and those which exercise the rest of the body. The breathing exercises are designed to establish conscious control over respiration as well as using the stomach muscles to ensure that the lungs are fully inflated.

The bodily exercises are performed very slowly and involve either stretching movements or the maintenance of particular positions for periods of time. Physiologically, the maintenance of posture utilizes the stretch reflex of muscles. The whole system can be likened to a cat stretching and rolling, with movements being slow and graceful. It is essential that these exercises become comfortable and patience is needed for this but, after three months' practice, many patients find they feel much better, fitter, and much less likely to develop headaches.

There are many techniques of teaching yoga. The meditation aspect of yoga is the most important so that those techniques controlling thought, or holding thoughts in the mind and so building on them, are likely to be of benefit in developing control.

Current approaches involve combining certain yoga techniques with biofeedback and it will be interesting to see how much this will achieve; it is conceivable that migraine patients who practise these techniques will not be so much at the mercy of stress and therefore will suffer fewer headaches.

Exercise

Exercise can bring on headaches in some people, but the reverse also obtains in that physical training can be of benefit in preventing headaches, possibly by 'toning up' the body and thereby the blood vessels. The effect of training on performance is well recognized: the heart and lungs work more efficiently so that we do not get out of breath so easily, the blood flow to muscles increases, and the muscles themselves become larger so that we do not get tired as readily. In the trained person, the heart beats more slowly at rest, and, during exercise, it does not beat as fast as before training nor does the blood pressure rise as high. A greater efficiency is achieved due to increased parasympathetic activity. The amount of noradrenalin and adrenalin released for a given amount of exertion decreases; in addition, supplies of energy become more readily available, which also helps to avoid fatigue.

When an untrained subject first starts exercising, the level of blood glucose drops, releasing hormones which break down stored supplies of sugar to raise the blood level. (In trained subjects, the blood sugar level shows an immediate rise on commencement of exercise.) Because training makes the body more efficient, it is more able to resist the effects of stress and the subject becomes able to do more during the day without getting tired.

Studies of the effects of exercise training on the frequency of headaches in migraine sufferers are producing encouraging results, possibly because the blood vessels alter their tone. Jogging, an activity becoming increasingly popular in both sexes, is the best sort of exercise for this purpose because it moves the greatest bulk of muscle and speeds up the heart rate. The distance and speed should be measured each time, the minimum number of runs being three times weekly. It is important to run fast enough to raise the pulse rate above 150 per minute and for long enough to make one slightly tired.

Physical methods

Acupuncture

In recent years the ancient Chinese technique of acupuncture has become increasingly used. Great claims have been made for the technique, particularly in the field of pain relief e.g. in patients undergoing major surgery with acupuncture anaesthesia.

The old Chinese teachings stated that the body consists of a balance of positive and negative forces, the *yin* and the *yang*, which flow through the body through various channels, along which there are special points where flow can be influenced. Particular points were thought to relate to specific organs. The acupuncturist feels many acupuncture 'pulses' and, through abnormalities in these, arrives at a diagnosis. Insertion of sharp needles into the appropriate combination of points are claimed to produce cessation of pain, as well as healing, in a particular organ.

There is no doubt that this technique can work as far as pain relief is concerned, but the evidence that it influences healing of disease is doubtful. The theoretical basis has no scienfitic substantiation—no-one has demonstrated the system of channels and points which are meant to cover the body, although there are areas of the skin with a decrease in electrical resistance (corresponding to acupuncture points).

We are then left with the question as to how pain is relieved. Legend has it that acupuncture was evolved following the observation by a soldier that the pain of his wound was relieved when he had been pierced elsewhere in his body by an arrow. In the heat of battle, adrenalin, noradrenalin, and cortisol are released into the blood stream; in addition, there is increased release of chemicals in the brain called peptides, particularly those involved in the appreciation of pain. This could explain how the body feels less pain when geared for a fight. The arrow wound could act, not only by its effect of further increasing the release of the pain-reducing substances, but also by another mechanism, by affecting the gating mechanism for pain (see Chapter 4). This theory explains how transmission of other sensations can block pain impulses, preventing them from ascending to consciousness. In effect, the pain gate can be shut by other sensations.

Acupuncture may work through similar mechanisms although the exact mode of action is unknown. Treatment by acupuncture sometimes needs to be fairly painful to be effective and, in some centres, a modified form of acupuncture is used passing a small electric current down the needles.

The usefulness of acupuncture in migraine has not yet been fully assessed. Theoretically the technique is useful for chronic pain but it is not so easy to see why it should be effective in a condition as episodic as migraine, although it has proved useful in the treatment of some cases of chronic migrainous neuralgia.

Counter-irritation

Similar in effect to acupuncture are various techniques which employ counter-irritation of the painful area. Some techniques use vibration and the patient stimulates the painful area for a few minutes each day. The efficacy of these techniques has yet to be assessed, particularly as they carry a potent placebo effect.

Manipulation

Manipulation of the spine, which may help backache, has been tried on patients with migraine, on the premise that the pain which arises at the back of the neck is brought about by malfunction of the cervical spine. No controlled trials have been done and the theoretical basis for this treatment is not scientifically proven.

Osteopathy is also based on spinal manipulation. Osteopaths ascribe a whole host of disorders to bad posture, e.g. disorders of digestion. Osteopaths are not recognized as medical practitioners in the U.K. by the General Medical Council, although in the United States their position is more accepted. Many medical schools there have recognized departments of osteopathy, and the course of studies is similar in length and content to that required for a medical degree.

Treatment without drugs

Although many of the claims for efficacy of manipulation are exaggerated, it has a place in treatment of certain conditions of the neck producing headache, by relieving muscle tension. Care must be taken because there are two vertebral arteries which run through the spine in the neck to supply the base of the brain; manipulation can lead to the blockage of these vessels causing a stroke.

Although many migraine patients claim to have had relief by osteopathic treatment, there is no clear-cut proof that this method has any higher percentage success rate than would be expected from the placebo response.

Treatment of allergy

In common parlance the term allergy is used to describe an unusual sensitivity but, strictly speaking, it should be confined to an altered reactivity on a second or subsequent exposure to a stimulus.

Some patients get headaches in response to an allergic reaction, possibly due to release of histamine. With the implication that food allergy plays a part in producing migraine, attempts have been made to desensitize patients to offending substances. This involves testing for allergy by using small amounts of suspected materials and noting those to which there is a response. This substance is then prepared in minute concentrations and increasing amounts are injected under the skin at frequent intervals in order to increase gradually the body's tolerance to it. This approach works well in hay fever and some cases of asthma, where there are definite identifiable allergic responses, but the situation in migraine is not as clear-cut. Although some migraine sufferers may have demonstrable food allergy, desensitizing them to the offending food does not always confer benefit. A trial of this form of treatment in a large number of people is needed, comparing results with those in another group of people who had been 'desensitized' with an ineffective substance. This sort of trial has not been undertaken and, in the present unsatisfactory situation, those with demonstrable allergy to a particular substance should take advice from specialists in the field, because of the possibility that they will experience some benefit from desensitization.

Physical methods of treatment during the migraine attack

In patients with infrequent or mild attacks cutting short the acute attack is all that is necessary. A variety of treatments are available and, although some are physical, most are based on the use of drugs (see next chapter).

A simple way to achieve relief is to compress the temporal artery on each side for several minutes; this decreases the pulsating pain and may induce vasoconstriction. Application of an ice pack to the head or immersion of the head in a cold bath may be beneficial, by the same mechanism. Ice packs specially designed for this purpose are now manufactured; alternatively, a plastic envelope filled with a gel which keeps cold for a long time can be kept in a refrigerator and taken out when needed.

Other patients find that vasodilating the extremities, by putting the feet in hot water, or immersion of the body in a hot bath, can be of benefit, since this also results in vasoconstriction of the scalp.

Temperature biofeedback, or hand-warming, has been tried in this context with some success. As previously described, a certain amount of apparatus is required and the usefulness of the technique is still controversial. A conscious attempt to vasoconstrict the temporal artery can also be attempted but it is difficult to prove the efficacy of this method. Many patients are not suited for concentration in this way, whilst others are not prepared to take the time and trouble to learn.

The two time-honoured relief measures are a darkened room and sleep, which can be as helpful as drugs.

8

Treatment with drugs

Most people are reluctant to take drugs. The two reasons given for this are side-effects and dependence.

Side-effects

There are very few medicines which are entirely free from unpleasant or harmful effects. If a drug works, it does so by acting on the body's tissues, so that when taken in excessive amounts, it will necessarily be harmful. People vary in their reactions, and some are more sensitive than others. Even the most widely taken drugs such as aspirin produce unpleasant effects, e.g. vomiting of blood in certain individuals, and most are familiar with the side-effects of the most popular of drugs—alcohol.

Dependence

Many drugs, particularly those having effects on the brain, such as sedatives and tranquillizers, have a reputation of dependence. This means that when the drug is stopped, the individual suffers from unpleasant withdrawal symptoms. The most well-known and dramatic of these is seen in chronic alcoholics and morphine addicts who, when their drug intake is suddenly stopped, develop hallucinations and tremor.

In chronic or recurrent disease, of which migraine is one example, it is particularly important to avoid dependence. The withdrawal symptoms seen after long-term administration of sedatives or tranquillizers are comparatively mild but can lead to insomnia, irritability, and depression.

For these reasons drugs should be taken only when necessary; the indication in migraine is when attacks are severe and interfere with daily life. When attacks are frequent, drug therapy may be more effective if preventive (prophylactic) treatment is given rather than waiting for the attacks which, when started, may not be so easily remedied.

Most people with migraine have mild attacks and the patients cope themselves without going to the doctor. It is only the severe migraine attacks, not controlled by the usual simple measures, that prove to be a treatment problem.

Treatment of the acute attack

The first phase (aura) of a migraine attack is vasoconstriction of the intracranial circulation. To prevent any possibility of damage to the brain due to cerebral ischaemia, the attack should be aborted before this phase but, once the first symptoms appear, vasoconstriction has already started. Occasionally people may get (prodromal) feelings the day before warning of an impending attack; these are sometimes related to gastric upsets, e.g. some people feel hungry, and eating sugar may abort the attack. In the majority of cases, the aim is to stop the headache coming and to prevent nausea and vomiting.

Pain itself has an effect on the cerebral vasculature; even mild pain causes an activation in the area of brain representing the painful area of the body and there is a slight increase in blood flow in that region. As pain increases, there is a more generalized increase in blood flow through the whole brain, caused by vasodilatation which in turn causes more pain. This cycle can be stopped by altering the appreciation of pain by means of analgesic (pain-killing) drugs; the feedback can also be broken by sedation using tranquillizing drugs such as Valium. Vasodilatation can be reversed using a short-acting vasoconstricting substance.

Nausea and vomiting are not only disturbing in themselves but they also upset and prevent the administration of remedies by mouth. These symptoms are partly due to a chemical transmitter acting on the 'vomiting centre' of the brain and partly due to the stomach becoming sluggish in its action

Treatment with drugs

(hypotonic). This means that the contents of the stomach, including tablets, do not readily pass down into the small intestine where most foods and medicines are absorbed. The reason why tablets taken during an attack of migraine do not help may be because they do not get into the blood stream. Sufferers often say: 'nothing helps the attacks, I just have to lie quietly in a darkened room and wait for it all to pass'.

Although the migrainous aura need not be very troublesome in itself, if it can be stopped, the full-blown attack may be prevented.

Most sufferers prefer to lie down during an acute attack. This is partly because it is difficult to function or concentrate as well during this time and also because lying down provides some relief of headache and nausea. Because light and sound are upsetting, a quiet darkened room is preferred.

Pain killers (analgesics)

Although it seems obvious that one of the best treatments for headache should be a pain-killer, different drugs have different mechanisms of stopping the pain. The most commonly used pain-killers, such as aspirin and paracetamol (Panadol), act mainly peripherally but also have some central actions on the brain, inhibiting the perception of pain. Another of their central actions is to act on the temperature regulatory mechanism and so reduce fever.

If taken early enough, many people find that aspirin or paracetamol will abolish an attack. Because absorption during a migraine attack is variable, it is better to take a soluble or effervescent form of these drugs, particularly in those prone to stomach problems, since ulcers are more likely to be aggravated by insoluble aspirin tablets.

Stronger analgesics act directly on the brain, by affecting the endorphin receptors and making the brain less responsive to pain; they often cause drowsiness or euphoria, and sometimes nausea. Most of these drugs are derivatives of opium and include pentazocine (Fortral), distalgesic, codeine, dihydrocodeine (DF 118), pethidine, diconal, morphine, and heroin. The last two should never be used in migraine but many people find codeine useful.

Most useful in attacks is a soluble combination of panadol and codeine (Paracodal, Solpadeine, etc.). This is the pain-killer of choice used in acute migraine clinics where 80 per cent of patients feel better within two hours.

Anti-emetics

It is useful to combine an analgesic with a medication which prevents nausea. Although there are many drugs acting against nausea, only one, metaclopramide (Maxolon), also has a specific action on the motility of the stomach, making it empty faster so that tablets or medicine will be passed into the small intestine and absorbed more quickly. This has been shown by measuring the levels of aspirin in the blood stream, which are twice as high after metaclopramide is given during the acute migraine attack. It should be given 15 minutes before other drugs to help absorption. Prochlorperazine (Stemetil) has a more powerful anti-nausea effect but does not affect the motility of the stomach. These anti-emetics are more effective when given by injection but this is not practicable in the home. Unfortunately the tablets may not be absorbed and metaclopramide is not available in suppository form. Some people prefer taking these medicines in the form of a syrup.

Perhaps the most effective popular remedy for migraine is a combination of an anti-emetic, paracetamol, caffeine and codeine known as Migraleve. This can be useful in the mild attack but is not quickly absorbed with more severe attacks.

Ergotamine

Some of the most effective remedies are drugs containing ergo-tamine although, like many other well-known drugs, the way in which this compound worked was unknown for many years.

Treatment with drugs

The drug comes from a mould that grows on rye; the name is derived from the French word 'ergot' meaning a 'spur' because part of the plant resembles a riding spur in shape. Eating bread made from mouldy rye can be poisonous, producing painful blue hands and feet ('St. Anthony's Fire'). As a result of such poisoning, whole villages in Eastern Europe were reported to have been visited by the devil and cure was obtained by visiting St. Anthony's shrine (which was in Egypt and outside the infected area). The use of ergotamine in the treatment of headache was first reported in Germany in 1883. In 1889, Dr. W. Thompson of the United States advised taking fluid extract of ergot by mouth but also suggested that rectal administration could be useful: 'As nausea is such a general accompaniment of this affection it is prescribed that if either of the doses be vomited it should be taken in an enema of two ounces of water. This medication rarely fails to arrest the attacks.' After this report, the use of ergot seems to have been forgotten, possibly because of the inconsistent effect of the extracts, until 1906, when an extract from ergot, *ergotoxine*, was isolated. This was later found to be a mixture of compounds. In 1918 a single compound was isolated—*ergotamine*—which was initially used to speed up uterine contractions during labour (ergot derivatives are still used in obstetrics). In 1925 ergotamine in its pure form was first used in the treatment of migraine and began to be prescribed widely. But it was not until 1937 that the main cause of the migraine headache was found to be due to blood vessels in the head becoming wider (extracranial vasodilation); and it was then shown that ergotamine worked because it narrowed these blood vessels (vasoconstrictor action). Because the migrainous aura was due to vasoconstriction, it was theoretically worrying to give a powerful vasoconstrictor drug at a time when vasospasm was present in the intracranial circulation. However, although ergotamine may prolong the migraine aura, there is no lessening of cerebral blood flow, possibly because the vessels at this time are less sensitive to the vasoconstrictive action of the drug.

77

Migraine

Ergotamine is usually safe and effective in the acute attack provided it is given in the correct dosage. Oral medication is simplest but often tablets taken during an acute attack may not be completely absorbed from the stomach so that the timing of the medication is critical.

Other vasoconstricting substances, such as caffeine, have been added to ergotamine to increase its efficacy, and this particular combination, e.g. Cafergot, can make oral intake as effective as an injection. Another compound commonly added to ergotamine is a drug effective against nausea and vomiting, e.g. cyclizine. For some sufferers with infrequent attacks, the combination is effective and remains the treatment of choice.

Ergotamine may also be given rectally, by injection, or by inhalation. Rectal administration can be effective when vomiting is a problem. This also applies to injections which, although usually given by a doctor, may be self-administered by the patients themselves but because ergotamine is a potentially addictive drug with adverse effects, this is not recommended. A more recent preparation of ergotamine is in the form of an inhaler which administers a measured dose of drug; although this gives rapid absorption and overcomes the joint problems of vomiting and overdosage, it has not yet become very popular.

About half the sufferers who take ergotamine have some sort of adverse reaction, e.g. nausea, shaking, trembling, and feeling weak. These side-effects may be so unpleasant that some sufferers prefer having migraine symptoms. In sensitive patients the levels of ergotamine in the blood can now be measured to see if there is a critical dose at which the migraine is relieved without side-effects. If these problems are overcome, ergotamine could still retain its position as the treatment of first choice for the acute migraine attack.

For the patient with occasional attacks of migraine, say about once every four months, ergotamine is still widely used, but those with more severe or more frequent migraine attacks require different methods because they can become addicted to ergotamine and need supervision in its withdrawal.

Treatment with drugs

Signs of ergotamine overdose include a chronic background headache with continuous nausea, made worse by increasing the usual dose. It can take two weeks of abstention before the situation is stabilized and the patient feels better.

Although ergotamine reduces the frequency of migraine attacks, it is dangerous if taken regularly or for too long as it can have toxic effects. One of the most dangerous of these is prolonged vasoconstriction which can cause gangrene. Ergot is related chemically to the powerful hallucinogenic drug lysergic acid diethylamide (LSD) so that it is not surprising that other side-effects of ergot include hallucinations and psychosis.

Another effect of chronic ergotamine ingestion is headache, which can be misinterpreted as being due to further migraine attacks so that more ergotamine is given. The headache of ergotamine overdosage is dull and nagging rather than the throbbing character of true migraine and it is not relieved by pain-killers. With ergotamine overdosage, stopping the drug leads to a worsening of the headache, but perseverence with not taking the drug will in almost all cases eventually lead to relief from this type of headache. People who attend migraine clinics are often suffering from this particular form of ergotamine addiction and it is difficult to break the habit. In order to avoid the vicious circle of ergotamine habituation, it is now not considered advisable to take ergotamine preparations if migraine attacks are frequent.

Dihydroergotamine

This has a lesser vasoconstrictive effect than ergotamine and is less effective during the acute attack although it is more frequently used as a preventive drug. It became available in 1943 but it is not used as widely in the U.K. as it is in the rest of Europe. The difference in drug usage between countries is of interest and even the way the drug is administered varies widely, depending on 'national character'. To generalize, the French like suppositories, the Italians prefer injections, and drops are preferred in Poland. It is possible that differences in dietary habit may have an effect on absorption and interaction of medication.

Many patients feel that their migraine attack is 'something from outside', and that calming down the headache only postpones the development of the full cycle; they feel that prevention of vomiting only prolongs the time during which they feel nauseated and that it is only after they vomit that they start to feel better. If this is true, then treatment may only prolong the suffering. The mechanism of such a reaction could be explained by a long-lasting chemical change lurking in the background which must be allowed to settle naturally, and it is only by careful study that the basis of the cyclical nature of migraine will be understood.

Although the most potent treatment for an acute attack may well be ergotamine, this drug can cause problems and, for this reason, an analgesic such as Paracodol together with an anti-emetic, such as Maxolon, is often preferable.

The fact that there are many medications used in the prevention of migraine attacks indicates not only that the production of migraine is highly complex with many stages at which intervention is possible, but also that no single drug is much better than the others. No two sufferers are the same and each patient needs to be treated as an individual. It may be necessary to try a variety of drugs in order to find the one that suits him best.

Preventive drugs

There are many types of drugs that can prevent migraine in sufferers who have frequent attacks. There would be little point in taking tablets every day if the attacks occur only once a year. Even monthly attacks, particularly when mild or responsive to simple remedies, should not require regular medication. It is when attacks occur several times a month and are interfering with life's ordinary activities that daily tablets may restore a patient to a normal life.

Treatment with drugs

The question of why some people and not others get migraine has been discussed in Chapters 3 and 5. To summarize the conclusions:

1. There can be little doubt that there is a familial tendency although its strength and the way in which migraine is inherited are still debatable. No drugs can alter this susceptibility.

2. There are predisposing or provocative factors which trigger an attack in a sensitive individual. These include factors such as stress, tension, or depression and drugs are very effective in relieving these factors.

3. Drugs can interfere with the biochemical changes that occur before or during a migraine attack (see Table 8.1).

External factors (stage I in Table 8.1)

Probably one of the commonest predisposing conditions in migraine is stress—anxiety, or tension. There are now many tranquillizing drugs which act to relieve these states and, in doing so, prevent migraine attacks. The most widely used group are the *benzodiazepines*, of which Valium and Librium are the best known and perhaps over-used. Tranquillizers exert a calming effect by acting on those structures in the brain concerned with emotion. (Apart from this effect on the specific receptors in the brain, Valium relaxes skeletal muscle, which is helpful in muscle-contraction headaches.) The soothing effect of these drugs on anxiety or agitation also makes people less likely to react to external stress and, because of this, it can be very effective in reducing the frequency of headaches.

Small doses are prescribed so that untoward effects, such as drowsiness, should not occur; other unwanted effects of Valium such as depression, apathy, and loss of muscle tone are also avoided. With chronic high dosage more serious effects are personality changes, such as sudden rages and irritability (similar to those experienced by people addicted

Migraine

Table 8.1

Diagram to show the genesis of a migraine attack with stages numbered in Roman numerals to indicate places where drugs may act (see text).

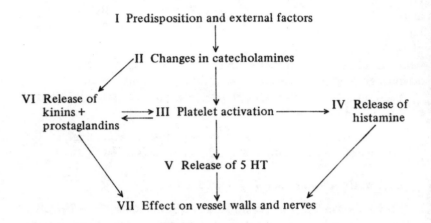

to alcohol). Suddenly stopping these drugs can result in acute episodes of anxiety. These serious side-effects are infrequent and Valium is a remarkably safe and very useful medicine. Other substances in this group include Ativan, Librium, and Nobrium.

Equally important in increasing the frequency of migraine is depression and this too is eminently remediable by anti-depressant drugs.

Of the three main types, the most commonly used are the *tricyclics*, e.g. Tryptizol (amitryptiline). These work by increasing the level of noradrenalin in the brain and so control mood. As the drug accumulates in the blood, it may take up to two weeks before its antidepressant effect is noticed. Because these drugs antagonize the neurotransmitter *acetyl-choline*, which helps to produce saliva, a common side-effect is dryness of the mouth. As acetylcholine is the transmitter

Treatment with drugs

of the parasympathetic nervous system, its other side-effects include speeding up the heart rate.

The tricyclics are surprisingly effective against migraine even in sufferers who are not depressed, possibly because the two conditions are related biochemically. If the migraine is aggravated by depression, treatment with tricyclics is particularly rewarding. Similar to the tricyclics but with fewer side-effects are the new tetracyclic antidepressants; although their value in migraine has not been fully assessed, they have the advantage that they exert their effects almost at once.

A second group of antidepressants act as inhibitors of the enzyme *monoamine oxidase* (MAO). This enzyme breaks down amines, active substances that play a part in the transmission of nervous impulses (neurotransmitters). MAO inhibitors are also effective in the treatment of migraine and their usefulness again is not confined only to patients who are depressed. This is paradoxical because the level of MAO is low during an attack of migraine; in this situation it is difficult to know in which way MAO is having its effect. However, there are several forms of MAO and more specific inhibitors, which inhibit only one variety, are now being tested.

Patients taking MAO inhibitors should not eat food containing tyramine (such as cheese) since they may develop reactions such as episodes of high blood pressure. Because of these reactions, the use of these drugs is limited to more serious cases of depression and they are not usually prescribed simply for migraine.

Drugs (stage I of Table 8.1)

L-Tryptophan. Although release of serotonin, 5-hydroxytryptamine (5HT), by blood platelets is an important factor in initiating migraine attacks, a lowering of 5HT in the brain may lessen tolerance to pain. In the brain, the nerve cells producing 5HT are generally inhibitory, i.e. they damp down nervous activity; this may explain why a lack of 5HT increases pain sensitivity. An obvious way to combat this would be to increase the concentration of 5HT but, unfortunately, when taken by mouth, it does not enter the brain. Another amino acid, L-tryptophan, does enter the brain where it is turned into 5HT by enzymes so that a large amount of L-tryptophan increases 5HT levels. (Mice fed on a diet deficient in L-tryptophan become intolerant to pain and dislike bright lights; this can be compared to the photophobia that causes migraine sufferers to wear tinted spectacles.) L-tryptophan is now being tried in the treatment of migraine; results are encouraging and further trials are planned. One great advantage of the drug is that there are no side-effects (except occasional drowsiness).

Clonazepam. This substance was first introduced as an anti-epileptic drug but is effective in migraine, particularly migrainous neuralgia where one tablet taken at night will alleviate the headache which often wakes people. The following case history demonstrates this point:

A 50-year-old, large man (about 6'3" tall and weighing 15 stone) was under a good deal of pressure at work and was also active as secretary of a number of voluntary organizations. One Christmas, he began to have attacks of severe pain behind the right eye, which went red, and his nostrils were blocked. The pain woke him and lasted for half an hour. He was unable to go to sleep again and was becoming increasingly tired.

The initial treatment was ergotamine three times daily for a limited period to try to break the pattern, but to no avail. Following this it was decided to try a trial of steroids, and Prednisolone was given three times daily (as this form of treatment sometimes works in this condition). This form of therapy can only be used for a short time and the course was stopped three weeks later; he was free of headaches for three weeks when they returned. He then took Clonazepam and the next day felt as if he were very drunk and was unable to move; on the following day he was still very sleepy but had not had a headache. He continued treatment on a smaller dose and the headaches disappeared, the only adverse effect being that he could be woken from his sleep.

Clonazepam can also be used in the treatment of acute attacks of common or classical migraine. There are some unwanted side-effects, the commonest being drowsiness. As well as having a direct and immediate sedative effect, it also increases the brain levels of 5HT but whether this is the reason why it is helpful in migraine is uncertain.

Lithium. Lithium, a light metal, acts on nerve fibres by being substituted for potassium which occurs naturally in the body and has an important role in the conduction of impulses along nerves. Lithium carbonate has been used in the treatment of mood changes for some years. It can be highly effective but the dose which controls severe depression is near to that at which unwanted effects appear, particularly shaking of the hands (tremor). For this reason, the level of lithium in the blood has to be carefully monitored.

More recently, success has been claimed for the use of this drug in much smaller doses (too small to affect depression) in the treatment of chronic migrainous neuralgia, the maximum success being achieved after about 30 weeks of treatment. It cannot yet be recommended for general use.

When a person is stimulated with a flashing light the brain produces a visual evoked response (see Chapter 6). If the intensity of the stimulus is increased, the brain can respond in one of two ways: the electrical response of the brain can increase (i.e. be augmented) or it can decrease (be reduced). Looked at simplistically, people can be divided into 'augmenters', who might be expected to be adversely affected by outside stimuli, and 'reducers', in whom the brain's response is damped down. In patients with manic depression there is a relatively high proportion of augmenters. Augmentation or reduction is not an inbuilt programmed form of response and treatment with lithium can turn an 'augmenter' into a 'reducer'. The change occurs at the same time as any improvement in the previous mental state. Work is now being done to see whether migraine patients in general turn out to be augmenters (see Chapter 9).

Peripherally acting drugs (stages II–VII in Table 8.1). The drug treatments so far outlined act on the centres for pain appreciation in the brain. There are other drugs which exert their action more peripherally on the migraine sequence, especially on the release from platelets of 5HT and other active substances.

Beta blockers (stage II in Table 8.1). Both adrenalin and noradrenalin play a part in the production of migraine, since they are produced by stress and affect the reactivity of blood vessels. This 'beta' action of adrenalin and noradrenalin (see also Chapter 4) can be countered by a group of drugs called beta blockers. In small doses these act mainly peripherally and will calm symptoms of anxiety and trembling, and lower a rapid pulse rate. Because beta adrenergic effects are of importance in migraine, beta blockers help prevent attacks and, for patients with a slightly elevated blood pressure, this may be the treatment of choice. Side-effects are few, although one form of beta blocker, *practolol*, had a serious side-effect on the eyes, and was recently withdrawn from the market. Other varieties do not cause this trouble and are commonly used for the control of blood pressure and prevention of angina.

Alpha blockers (stage II in Table 8.1). Blocking the alpha effects of noradrenalin on the blood vessel wall would also be expected to be useful in the treatment of migraine, by inhibiting the initial vasoconstriction and thus preventing the attacks from developing. Alpha blockade is not as easily produced as beta blockade but recently a new drug, *indoramine*, has been introduced for this purpose. Recent trials suggest that it may be useful in reducing the frequency, intensity, and duration of migraine attacks.

Drugs are now available which block both alpha and beta receptors. At present they are used only in the treatment of high blood pressure, but if early morning migraine is related to the surge of noradrenalin noticed two hours before waking, then blocking the effect of that release should prevent the headache appearing. Although there has not yet been any scientific report of this approach, a few patients are currently taking this preparation.

Aspirin (stage VI in Table 8.1). This is the commonest pain reliever and nearly every one has taken this drug, but only in recent years has the way it works been found out: it acts by preventing the formation of prostaglandin, a naturally occurring fat with a wide variety of actions (see Chapter 5, p. 48). Other drugs besides aspirin work in this way and include a variety of antirheumatic drugs such as *indomethacin, phenylbutazone, ibuprofen,* and *Anturan.* Many migraine sufferers show a good response to these drugs, the headaches being lessened in intensity and frequency when these compounds are used prophylactically.

Trials have started to assess the value of *sulphinpyrazone* (Anturan) in the treatment of migraine. This type of drug can be used when food allergy causes migraine.

Antihistamines (stage IV in Table 8.1). Anti-inflammatory substances used by migraine sufferers include indomethacin, an antirheumatic agent, and *disodium cromoglygate,* a substance that prevents the release of histamine and other substances concerned with inflammation and proven to be effective in asthma and hay-fever (see stage IV in Table 8.1). Platelets release histamine as well as 5HT. Many people with hay-fever take antihistamines, which act by preventing the effect of histamine on tissues, e.g. inflammation and irritation of the lining of the nose, eyes, and throat. There are a number of other compounds used in migraine which have anti-5HT effects and antihistamine effects.

The part histamine plays in the production of migraine attacks is uncertain and results with antihistamine preparations have been disappointing except in cluster headaches and in some patients whose migraine may be allergic in origin.

Pizotifen (Sanomigran) (stages IV and V in Table 8.1). This is a powerful anti-5HT agent, as well as antihistamine. After two weeks of taking the standard dose of three tablets a day, about 80 per cent of patients will notice a lessening of the frequency of migraine headaches. There is a mild antidepressant effect and another benefit is that any concomitant allergies are improved.

A 27-year-old casualty doctor found that he began to have severe migraine attacks every week. The headaches used to begin behind his right eye, which became red and watered. Instead of the pain lasting a short time, as in cluster headache, there would then ensue a severe headache lasting many hours which was accompanied by vomiting. This made it extremely difficult to work the long hours expected and he felt guilty when his friends had to 'cover' for him during a migraine. Examination revealed no abnormality and he began to take pizotifen. Within two weeks the headaches stopped and he was able to pass a stiff examination shortly afterwards. He suffered from hay fever but reported that, although the pollen count was high, this had also disappeared. After six months the treatment was phased out and the headaches did not return.

Half the patients who are helped by this treatment do not get a recurrence of headaches once treatment has stopped. It is as if the blood vessels 'unlearn' their previous pattern of response and no longer go through the variations in calibre associated with the migraine attack.

There are two main unwanted effects with this drug. The first is drowsiness, so that the manufacturers advise care when driving, and suggest that alcohol is not drunk while on treatment, a caution that also applies to other anti-5HT, as well as antihistamine, agents. The other effect is that about one-third of patients put on weight of the order of half a stone, because inhibiting 5HT in the brain (which happens to a slight extent) increases the appetite.

Methysergide (Deseril) (stage V in Table 8.1). Another very potent inhibitor of 5HT is methysergide, which is an effective anti-migraine prophylactic. Prolonged use may lead to fibrous thickening of certain structures such as the kidneys, so that this therapy should not be prolonged for more than three months at a time, an interval of one month being required before another course can be started.

Treatment with drugs

Clonidine (stage VII in Table 8.1). This drug was first used in the treatment of high blood pressure and it acts both on the brain and on blood vessels. Centres in the brain which control blood pressure are affected in such a way that they cause blood vessels to dilate, while the blood vessels themselves are made less responsive to noradrenalin; both of these effects serve to reduce blood pressure.

In smaller doses, clonidine should prevent many of the chemical changes which spark off a migraine attack; Dixarit, its proprietary name, contains about a quarter of the dose of clonidine used for high blood pressure. When, in this dosage, it prevents migraine, it works well, but people who do not benefit from initial treatment will not benefit with increasing dosage.

Although several trials have found that clonidine confers no benefit when compared to a placebo, some physicians find it useful in certain circumstances, as the almost total lack of side-effects often make it a drug of first choice in prophylaxis, especially in women whose migraine attacks occur at the time of the menstrual periods. Like other preventive drugs, it may take up to two weeks for the effects to become manifest.

A group of medical students were given Dixarit or a placebo prior to a party in which the intake of wine and cheese was excessive. The next morning the Dixarit-treated group developed headache significantly less often than the placebo treated group. This result, although not scientifically reported, is interesting because cheese and red wine are most potent in producing headaches. Tyramine is only one of these factors present in red wine. The 'hangover' headache is due to a variety of factors, one of which is that the alcohol dehydrates the brain tissue to give low pressure headache (see Chapter 2). Some of the chemicals in alcoholic drinks have effects on their own, acting to cause a vascular headache of the migraine type. The part that an excess of tobacco plays in the hangover headache is uncertain but nicotine is a well-known precipitant of headache.

The main compounds to influence platelet activation are

called thromboxanes. These are derived from one of the fatty substances which may trigger a migraine attack. These free fatty acids are converted into substances (pro-aggregating agents) which eventually cause the platelets to clump together. These also cause constriction of vessel walls, which react by producing substances with opposite actions (i.e. they convert the free fatty acids into inhibitors of platelet aggregation and into powerful dilators of vessel walls).

Altering these compounds in the body should in theory have a marked effect on migraine, especially if platelet activation could be prevented without changing the size of blood vessels. Constriction of the vessel wall is the first part of the migraine cycle and breaking this pattern would be therapeutically helpful. Most substances which inhibit the production of thromboxanes in the platelets also inhibit the production of anti-aggregating substances in the vessel walls as both have similar initial production stages. Preventing dilatation—the cause of the pain—will produce relief by the same mechanism as the many vasoconstrictor medicines which are effective during an acute attack of migraine.

9

The future

Migraine clinics

The realization that migraine is a disorder causing a vast
amount of unnecessary suffering has led to an increased
interest in the subject. Specialist centres have been set up
with the support of the Migraine Trust for treatment and research of acute migraine attacks in London (the two clinics
serving this purpose are the Princess Margaret Clinic and the
Charing Cross Hospital Migraine Clinic). In addition to offer-
ing treatment of the acute attack, these and other clinics
provide consultation facilities for general practitioner refer-
rals, so that all sorts of treatment methods are tried and
many trials undertaken.

Perhaps the most important function of the migraine clinic
is to deal with and study the acute attack which, surprisingly,
is rarely seen by most hospital doctors. In the clinic, tests can
be performed on those with an acute attack which, it is
hoped, when pieced together will give a better idea of what
happens during the acute attack. This insight should help in
the development of more appropriate treatment.

These studies are also important in the assessment of treatment. For instance, the recognition that tablets taken during
an attack do not always help led to the measurement of levels
in the blood of aspirin taken during an attack; these were
shown to be lower than when taken at any other time. It was
this finding that confirmed the slowness of emptying of the
stomach and the consequent recommendation to use Maxolon
to stimulate the gut and aid absorption, so making the levels
of ingested drugs higher.

The advantage of grouping patients with the same disorder
together is that it allows the clinic staff to concentrate on

specialized areas and makes research easier. The facility for treatment of acute attacks helps not only patients but research workers. However, in countries where patients visit a specialist, a neurologist, directly rather than being referred on from their general practitioner, there is not such a demand for such clinics. This means that research workers do not have the opportunity of studying patients during an acute attack.

A town (or catchment area of population) has to be of a particular size in order for such facilities to be viable, e.g. about a quarter of a million people is probably the smallest size for this purpose. Alternatively, there needs to be a large concentration of commuter workers in the area (as there is in the City of London where the Princess Margaret Clinic is situated).

In the United States there are several organizations operating such clinics which, although privately run, are fully used.

The ideal migraine clinic would have a neurologist in attendance because the causes of headache not due to migraine need to be diagnosed. The investigative facilities for this would be required, in addition to facilities for more elaborate tests needed in research or in treatment, such as the measurement of factors in the blood as 5-hydroxytryptamine (5HT), adrenalin, noradrenalin, and monoamine oxidase (MAO). A clinical pharmacologist, an expert in the use of drugs, should also be available to advise on dosage and administration and the setting up of trials of new medications. In addition to consultation rooms, there should be an acute treatment area where the atmosphere should be quiet and relaxed with facilities for excluding light and sound-proofing. Lying down and relaxing in such an atmosphere can be very helpful in therapy.

Ideally there would be short-stay facilities; some hospitals have sleep laboratories where the patient is put in a single room and can be assessed using laboratory apparatus such as an EEG machine so that changes occurring during sleep can be monitored. Studies like this led to the finding that noradrenalin levels rose one to two hours before waking up in

The future

those who suffered from early morning migraine (when they generally wake from REM (rapid eye movement) sleep). The first observation was obtained by continuous blood sampling from a tube in an arm vein; since the needle was kept in the vein, no further pain or discomfort was experienced by the patient and only small amounts of blood samples were necessary.

The EEG changes during sleep are specific for the various stages. By EEG monitoring from leads attached to the patient's head, researchers were enabled to see which stage of sleep the patient had reached. REM sleep is so called because in this stage there are rapid eye movements, and dreaming occurs. During dreaming there are the same glandular responses in the body as are obtained during the same real activities, e.g. running for a 'bus in a dream causes the heart to beat faster and this is associated with a rise in noradrenalin levels. The rise in noradrenalin levels before an early morning migraine may be related to dreams caused by stresses during waking life. Other advantages of overnight accommodation are treatment for those whose headache has not responded to out-patient treatment, for assessing new treatments under controlled conditions, and for investigating precipitating factors such as dietary factors with full biochemical monitoring.

Migraine clinics are expensive, since some blood tests can cost £3–4 each, whilst an EEG machine can cost several thousands of pounds, and apparatus needed to equip a laboratory for biochemical investigation could cost up to £40 000. The salaries of medical, nursing, secretarial, and technical staff could cost a further £50 000 a year. It is difficult to obtain these sums of money for a disease that is not fatal and does not have as great an appeal to charity as more dramatic diseases.

There is no doubt that a number of people from different disciplines working on the same problem, with sufficient funds can do a lot more in research than separate groups working independently.

Migraine

Research funds

Britain has the advantage that research is cheaper than else-where, partly because of the comparatively low level of salaries on an international scale. This is not the only reason why many multinational pharmaceutical firms do much of their basic research in this country: the U.K. has a high inter-national reputation for medicine.

One important task for those working on migraine is dis-tributing information about treatment to those concerned. There is evidence of a growing interest in the condition. As with many other disorders, migraine sufferers in this country have formed patient associations, e.g. the Migraine Trust and the British Migraine Association in the U.K., and the National Migraine Foundation in the U.S.A. The Migraine Trust is a charitable body that distributes information about migraine in the form of a Newsletter, a publication in the form of a paperback on migraine, a letter-answering service and sup-port of research throughout the U.K.

Applications for research money are studied by the Trust's medical advisers and many projects are currently being funded. Every two years the Trust organizes an International Migraine Symposium at which experts from all over the world gather and the report of their research activities into all aspects of the migraine problem is later published. The money to fund these activities is raised from private dona-tions and fund-raising activities. The Research Group on Mi-graine and Headache of the World Federation of Neurology also meets regularly and the last open meeting, held in Amsterdam in October 1977, was well attended, indicating the worldwide scientific interest in the problems of head-ache in general and migraine in particular.

Why is research so slow?

There are two ways in which research can be undertaken. The first, the so-called 'target-directed' approach, depends on a commercial attitude, often seen in industry where a problem is stated and a scientific team has to solve it. There is no doubt that while orientated research has produced many advances, it usually creates strong pressure to cut corners and appear to make more progress than is actual, so that the quality of research may not be up to the highest standards.

The alternative method is the academic approach which allows freedom to scientists and is not concerned with the financial or administrative basis. In this long-cherished approach towards research, often followed by universities, the scientist has total freedom to pursue whatever lines of research he or she chooses, hoping that from this something may emerge. Although some useless work may be done, this attitude to research is necessary since it may open unexpected doors: the scientist does not rush down a motorway to his destination, but stops to look at the scenery, which may be more revealing.

Many useful factors about migraine have come to light from other disciplines peripheral to migraine research, for example, the research into platelets, mental illness, and gastro-enterology have all produced results of value in the understanding of migraine.

New drugs

Scientific 'breakthroughs' are exceptional and are, in spite of the name, usually built on slowly built-up theories. The same applies to the development of new treatments. Once a biochemical change has become established in the causation of a sequence relevant in production of headache, ways can be found to block these changes. There may be 200 similar compounds capable of doing this, and each has to be tested in animals first for efficacy and side-effects. A compound may have too weak an effect, or have an effect that is too short-lived. The search can go on for years, and finally, when a promising compound is found, toxicity studies need to be undertaken, again first in animals. Any hint that the drug

95

causes cancer or can affect the foetus leads to its being rejected.

Once toxicity studies have ended, pilot studies in human volunteers can be undertaken, during which efficacy is observed and side-effects noted. These trials have to be approved by the Government. After this comes large-scale drug trials and only then general release of the drug. All these processes can take up to twenty years so that it is amazingly expensive for a pharmaceutical company to produce a new drug.

The nature of migraine

Evidence has been presented which indicates that there are differences between those who suffer from migraine and those who do not. It is not yet known how much these differences are secondary to the development of chronic recurrent headaches, e.g. the platelet abnormalities could easily be secondary to stress. These disturbances, noted even before the aura starts, are sometimes related to disturbances of hormonal or hypothalamic function but it is unknown why the hypothalamus behaves like this. The cause of the phasic quality of attacks— for example some people wake up and know they are going to have a migraine if, for instance, they eat cheese on that day— is also of interest. On what does this fluctuating tendency depend?

There may be some variation in the activity of platelet MAO which makes the migraine patient more susceptible to amines at various times. The cause of these fluctuations could be biological clocks which affect the cycles of hormones; in women, the menstrual cycle is one obvious example. The responsiveness of the nervous system to stimulation is another factor which could vary from day to day but its control mechanism is also unknown, although 5HT may in some way be connected.

Treatment with lithium can change a person from being an 'augmenter' into a 'reducer' on the visual evoked response (VER) test (see Chapter 8). It is possible that migraine suf-

The future

ferers tend to be augmenters, but this needs to be tested. Possibly they become augmenters when a migraine is due and are reducers the rest of the time. The latency differences in VER between migraine patients and controls need re-study. The mechanism of this effect has to be clarified, especially if it is due to neurotransmitter changes. This would sustain the hope that the changes can be rectified.

The observations that migraine sufferers respond differently to hormonal stress and that their blood vessels differ in reactivity from 'normals' also requires confirmation.

The attack itself poses many questions. Why, for instance, does there seem to be a cycle which in some people has to run its full length? In these people, drugs only delay the ending, making the symptoms drag on for days. What is this abnormality which persists and is more potent than some of our strongest drugs? Does it really depend on disordered platelet function? There is evidence that platelets in migraine patients are hyperaggregable, and that they may aggregate more during an attack. The release of 5HT cannot be responsible for the whole cycle, since the 5HT released decreases very rapidly. Evidence for the changes is still speculative.

Treatment

Treatment needs more study. The acute attack is now readily treatable, in the clinic at least. What is needed is more work into orally absorbable compounds which act quickly and effectively. Drug prophylaxis is becoming more widely used. Of most interest will be the drugs which control 5HT levels, those which prevent allergic reactions occurring, and anti-platelet drugs. Since any drug is 95 per cent effective at the most and this still leaves 5 per cent of sufferers, a wide choice of different medications may well be useful.

Also of interest will be the physical methods such as biofeedback and methods which enable the patient to control his own bodily functions. Migraine, like high blood pressure, would appear to lend itself *par excellence* to this sort of approach. Because of side-effects it is undesirable to treat what is in effect a life-long problem with drugs.

Appendix

RELAXATION EXERCISES

General introduction

The doctor should make sure you are comfortable and supported. He should outline the theory of relaxation and explain why you should learn to relax. This should be followed by a short explanation of the system used—and examples of the best method to follow—with the reassurance that it is easy and individually tailored.

Exercises: contraction and relaxation

Lie on your back on the floor, with your head on a pillow

tense your whole body . . . (e.g. muscles, stomach muscles, facial muscles, etc.) and relax
take a deep breath in and let it out with a sigh
Repeat once more

Tense your left leg, raising it slightly off the floor
feel the tension throughout your leg (in your ankle, your calf, your knee, your thighs)
feel discomfort . . . and relax
feel that the leg is heavy on the floor,
heavy and relaxed
Repeat—with right leg
Now let the floor take all the weight of your legs. There should be no more tension—they are completely relaxed.

Hunch your shoulders up to your ears. Feel the tension down your spine, across your back, in your neck . . . and then relax.

Tense your right arm, raising it slightly off the ground.
Clench your fist, tighten and rotate your wrist, feel the tension in your forearm, your elbow, and upper arm . . . then relax
Let the arm rest heavily on the floor, completely relaxed
Repeat—with right arm

Migraine

There should be no more tension in your arms or your legs. The floor should take all their weight, heavy and relaxed.

Raise your head off the pillow and turn it as far to the left as possible —now to the right, feeling the tension; back to the centre—and let it fall on to the pillow—heavy and relaxed. There should be no tension in your neck at all. Your head is resting heavily on the pillow.
Take a deep breath in and let it out with a sigh.

Now tense the muscle of your buttocks—pull in as hard as you can . . . and relax

Arch your back off the floor slightly: feel the contraction and tension right through your spine, and relax. . . .
Take a deep breath in and let it out with a long sigh.

Now tense your stomach; pull in the muscles so hard that you can feel the tension in your chest as well. Hold it till it almost hurts, and relax.
Take another deep breath in and let it out with a long sigh

Now your whole body should be heavy and relaxed; completely supported by the floor. There is no tension anywhere, no discomfort. You feel heavy and relaxed.

Now relax the facial muscles. First frown as hard as you can, drawing your brows as close together as possible, and then relax. Feel your forehead smoothing out.
Screw up your eyes as tightly as possible, feel the discomfort—and relax Leave your eyelids slightly closed. Feel the eyes heavy in their sockets— heavy and relaxed.
Clench your jaw and push your tongue against your lower teeth—feel the discomfort of tension. Relax, let the jaw drop slightly and your tongue drop behind your lower teeth. Feel all your facial muscles smooth and relaxed.

Suggestion therapy

Say to yourself:
I feel my legs growing heavier and heavier and more relaxed. There is no tension right through from my ankles to my hips. Heavy and relaxed.

I feel my arms growing heavier and heavier. My hands are heavy, wrists are loose. The floor takes all their weight.

100

Appendix

My head is heavy on the pillow, heavy and relaxed.
There is no tension down my spine or across my shoulders.
My whole body is relaxed and supported.

My forehead feels broad and smooth.
The space between my eyes seems very wide, and all tension around my
eyes and round my mouth has gone.

My jaw is relaxed.
All my facial muscles are at rest—relaxed.
I am completely relaxed.
And while my body is relaxed, I try to let my mind relax, too.

Glossary of terms

Acetylcholine: A chemical acting at the junction between nerves and muscles and in the parasympathetic nervous system (*see also* neurotransmitter)

Allergy: Altered reactivity of the body to a foreign substance. Allergies are usually mediated by immunological (*see below*) mechanisms.

Alpha receptor: One of the receptors (active sites) stimulated by adrenalin and noradrenalin.

Amine: A substance which has an amine ($-NH_2$) group as part of its chemical structure. Amines act as neurotransmitters (*see below*) and include adrenalin, noradrenaline, 5-hydroxytryptamine (5HT), tyramine, phenylethylamine, and dopamine.

Analgesic: A drug that relieves pain.

Aura: A term used to describe premonitory symptoms of either migraine or epilepsy.

Benzodiazepines: A group of drugs used as tranquillizers, e.g. Valium, Mogadon, Dalmane.

Beta receptor: One of the receptors stimulated by adrenalin.

Biochemistry: The study of the chemical reactions which take place in the body (literally: the chemistry of life).

Biofeedback: The term for relaying back information, usually into the conscious mind, regarding an automatic function. By using this technique it is hoped that these unconscious processes can be brought under voluntary control.

Catecholamine: An amine containing the catechol structure, often acting as a neurotransmitter, e.g. adrenalin.

Cerebrospinal fluid: The fluid which bathes the brain and spinal cord.

Cortex: The grey matter that forms the outer part of the brain substance.

Cranial nerves: The twelve pairs of nerves which arise from the brain itself. Their functions are:

I	smell	VIII	hearing and balance
II	vision	IX	palatal movement, taste
III, IV, and VI	eye movements	X	parasympathetic function
V	sensation of face, chewing	XI	some shoulder muscles
VII	facial muscles	XII	tongue movements

Electroencephalography (EEG): The recording of the electrical activity of the brain using suitable amplifiers.

Electromyography (EMG): The recording of the electrical activity of muscles and the speed of transmission of a nerve impulse.

Endoperoxide: A chemical that can produce other active substances such as thromboxane (*see below*) and prostacylin (*see below*).

Encephalin: peptide (*see below*) with pain-relieving activity.

Glossary

Enzyme: A biological substance which speeds up chemical reactions.

Epilepsy: An attack caused by abnormal electrical activity in the brain and consisting either of involuntary movements of the body or loss of consciousness. It can be either inherited or acquired due to a structural abnormality of the brain (e.g. stroke, tumour).

Erythrocyte sedimentation rate (e.s.r.): A blood test which aids in the diagnosis of inflammation.

Free fatty acids (FFA): Fats found in the blood that are released in conditions of stress which the body can use for energy.

Frontal lobe: The front part of each cerebral hemisphere.

Hemianopia: Blindness of half of a visual field.

Hemisphere: One side of the brain.

Hormone: A chemical substance which controls certain functions of the body.

Immunology: The study of the body defence systems against foreign proteins e.g. germs (microorganisms). White blood cells are of two types: one, called lymphocytes, produces antibodies which cause foreign substances to be cleared from the circulation or make them more likely to be engulfed by the second type, called polymorphs, which act as scavengers. An inappropriate immune response can damage the body (allergy).

Ischaemia: Lack of blood to a body tissue.

Kinin: A chemical substance, which, among other actions, may increase pain and is associated with inflammatory activity.

Lithium: A light metal, whose salt is used as a tranquillizer, particularly in dampening mood swings. It is also used in the treatment of chronic migrainous neuralgia.

Monoamine oxidase (MAO): An enzyme which helps in the breakdown of catecholamines (*see above*).

Monosodium glutamate: A substance used to increase the flavouring of foods (especially drinks).

Neurone: A nerve cell.

Neurotransmitter: A chemical which passes an impulse between two adjoining nerve cells (synapse; *see below*).

Occipital lobe: The back part of the brain concerned with vision.

Parasympathetic nervous system: One of the two parts of the 'autonomic' nervous system. Acetylcholine (*see above*) is the main neurotransmitter utilized. Activation of this system causes, among other changes, the heart to slow and the pupils to constrict.

Parietal lobe: The area of the cerebral hemisphere midway between the frontal and occipital areas.

Peptide: A chemical that forms part of a protein molecule, and may have marked activity on the nervous system.

Physiology: The study of the functional organization of the body (neurophysiology – of the nervous system).

Placebo: A substance without pharmacological effect, but which does in fact seem to help certain conditions, especially pain. Although previously thought to be due to suggestion, recent work suggests that there may be an activation of encephalins (*see above*).

Glossary

Platelet: A very small blood cell which plays an important part in clotting and stores many chemical substances including 5HT (*see* amine).

Prostacyclin: A derivative of arachidonic acid (an FFA) produced by the vessel wall; although very short lived, it has potent anti-aggregating and vaso-dilating (*see below*) actions.

Scotoma: A blind spot in the field of vision.

Stroke: A disturbance of the brain due to either blockage or rupture of a blood vessel.

Sympathetic nervous system: One of the two parts of the autonomic system. The main transmitter is noradrenalin. Activation causes an increase in heart rate and a widening of the pupils.

Synapse: The 'join' between two nerves. Nervous impulses are transmitted across the gap by release of chemicals called neurotransmitters (*see above*).

Temporal arteritis: (cranial arteritis): An inflammatory condition of blood vessels which is characterized by severe continuous headache and occurs only in the elderly.

Thromboxane: An unstable, highly potent chemical produced by platelets and having marked platelet aggregating, and vasoconstricting (*see below*) activity. It is derivative of arachidonic acid (one of the FFAs (*see above*)).

Tricyclics: A class of antidepressant drug (so called because their basic chemical structure consists of three rings).

Trigeminal nerve: Fifth cranial nerve; literally 'three turns' because it has three divisions, ophthalmic, maxillary, and mandibular.

Ventricle: Space within the brain containing cerebrospinal fluid.

Vasoconstriction: Constriction of a blood vessel.

Vasodilatation: Expansion of the diameter of a blood vessel.

Index

Index

Index